# WHISPERS IN THE CURRENTS

## A POETRY COLLECTION

### WHISPERS
### BOOK ONE

## CHRISTIE LEIGH BABIRAD

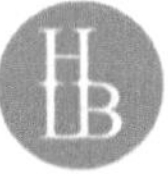

*Whispers in the Currents is dedicated to my brother, Robert Babirad. "Robbie," my most favorite person to travel with, and the person who always encourages and inspires me to adventure and live my life to the fullest.*

# PERSPECTIVE

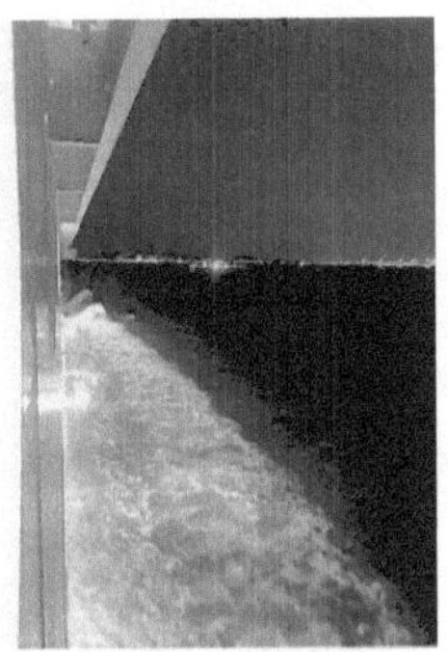

Until you've been busking across the country,
All to sing the songs inside of you,
Lost your mama,
Lost your father,
Half-blind with a tear-stained smile still on your face,
I can't manage to care about the imperfections you see
in me.

I saw an inspiring man on the television last night
And thought—
We're all simply trying to leave our mark here before
our time is up.
Could be fifty years from now.
Could be tomorrow.
No matter the time,
I don't have a moment to be judged by someone,
Who as far as I can see,
Has lived much less than him or me.

# Since I Took This Chance

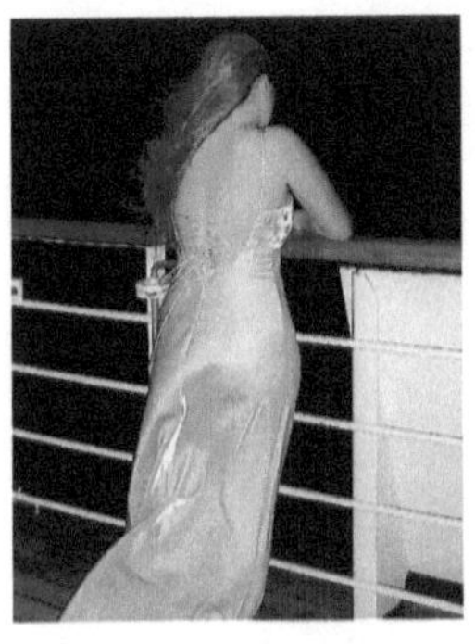

I have words to write again.
The curtains are pulled back.
Windows are open wide.
A romantic hazy summer sun beams in.
Hope enters through a confetti of tiny hearts dancing
inside me.

A strong and gentle hand reaches out to my still hesitant one.
Blue and brown eyes shine into each other.
At the beach we watch the waves curl up and down,
Some swiftly sliding into the shell-covered sands,
Others loudly crashing the shore.
Salt air fills my senses.
My flurry of emotions becomes steady with confidence.
And I know,
This is an adventurous and uncalculated love.
All I ever wanted,
All for me,
Since I took this chance with you.

# ABBY

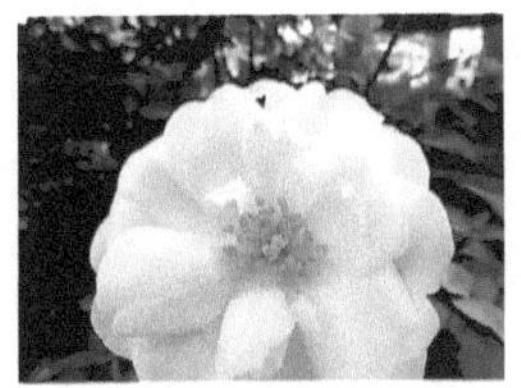

She was afraid of the clowns,
This tough and witty little girl.
She curled up in my lap,
A mess of tangled brown hair,
From playtime to tears.

She chose me to protect her from what she feared.
Her head rested against my chest,
I had never felt a grander purpose.
Thinking on how harsh this life can be,

As one goes from this age to where I am now.

How comforting it is to have moments of connection,
Where we feel deeply loved and protected.
One hand rested on her warm head,
The other hand on her back,
I said, "Everything is going to be okay," simultaneously
sending a prayer up to Heaven for this to be true.

# Between Two Worlds

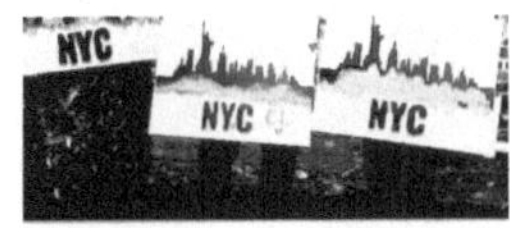

When your thoughts tug between voicing past or
present tense.
Any moment could be the call you were never waiting
for.
Emotions flare from tears to anger to desire—
There has to be a way to turn this around,
This can't be real.
And questions of the faith you claimed bubble to the
surface.

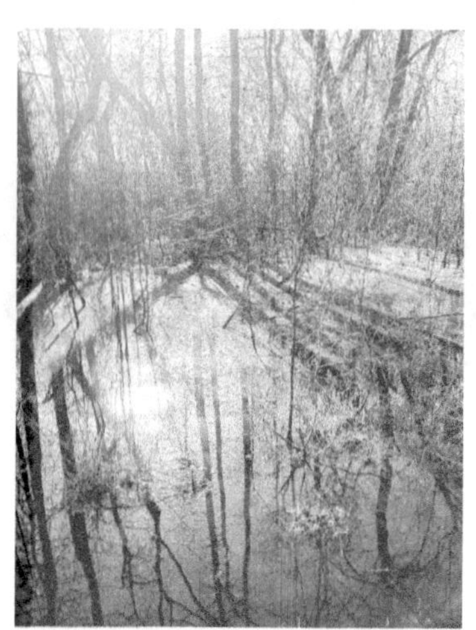

# YOUR CALLS

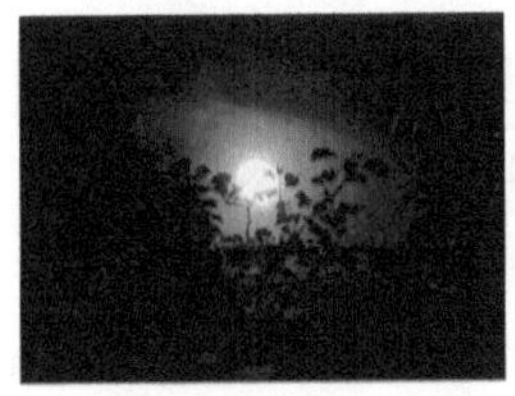

You didn't place the stories inside me,
But demanded I know they were already there.
Checking in.
Touching base.
I'd rush to the phone knowing if I missed you,
You'd already be on to your next chase.
"I'll call on Sunday," your messages would say.
When Sundays came,
Under the moonlight of my yard,
Our conversations would take me to the richest spaces,

Deeply into scarlet rose gardens
And tales of ancient caves of mysteries you would
relay.
You were never here nor gone,
Yet you possessed an uncanny earthly passion.
You sought to connect with everything and everyone.
Now you have taken off to an exceptionally unreach-
able place,
Without any warning or footprints I could trace,
Only memories I hold tightly to.
And Sundays you're still on my mind.
And I still wait for you,
Between the grand adventures
I'm sure you're flying off toward.
I wait for a sign or synchronicity from you.
And before each new idea and move I make,
I still hold a moment for you.
I still always think of you.

# A Different World

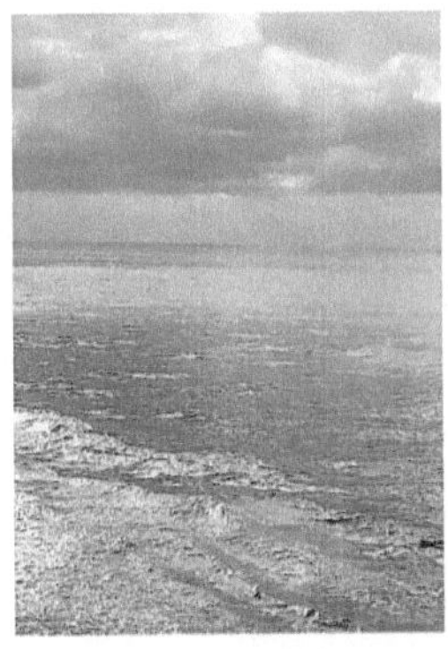

This world is an exceptionally cruel place for some.
Always has been.
I hope this won't always be.
The targets change and shift.
The cruelty stays the same.
And I pray.

I empathetically pray for these scorned souls.
I wish for them to be in the most radiant castles of
Heaven now.
I wish for them to be filled with the love they never
received here on Earth.
And I pray.
I deeply pray they have the power to send conscious
compassion down to us all,
Because we can never have too much,
Especially filling with light those most damaged and
fearful souls among us.

# Questioning Heart

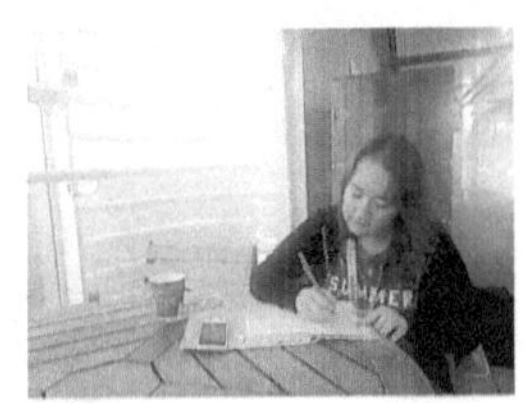

What do I have to say?
Here in this journal of mine,
thinking about you,
wishing you would have come my way by now,
because I believe in the stars aligning,
destiny
I have made a friend of mine,
and my faith speaks still,
reassurances,
my soul will not be left half-full.

# THROUGH YOUR LENS

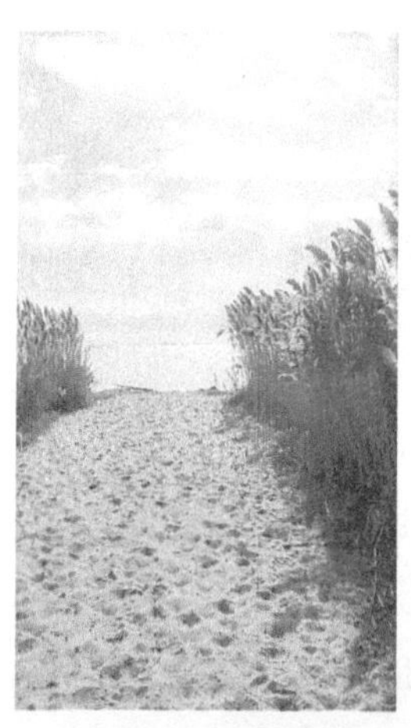

I'll come back when everything is blooming for me.
I already have you on my schedule, you see.
I had to put you out of my mind.
I had to cut the ties for what I needed to find.
Your story wasn't traveling a path I could see.

I'm inspired by practical steps that lead to all I long to be.

I'll come back when our differences can blend if you choose to see them.

However, I do understand if the time apart will have changed your heart for me.

# When Doubt Shakes This House

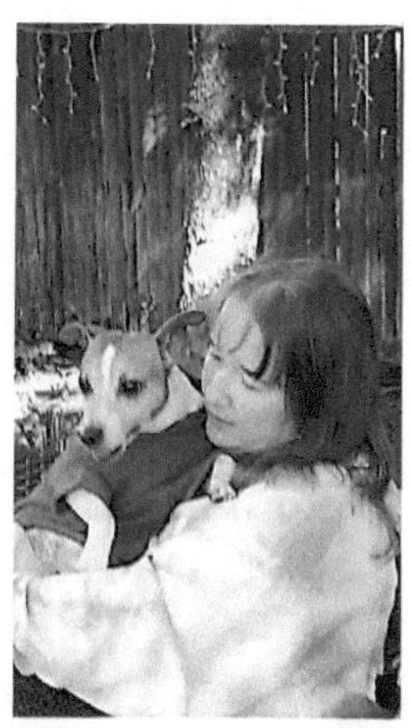

Every morning she battles creatures in her mind,
holding up pictures of how her life should look,
like skating judges taking in her every move.

Every night there is another crew

reminding her of the fears of losing all that matters
most to her,
like that "friend" who always questions her momen-
tary joy.

Yet every day she puts one foot in front of the other,
taking hold of each moment and doing her best,
like real love has always encouraged her to do.

# GRACE

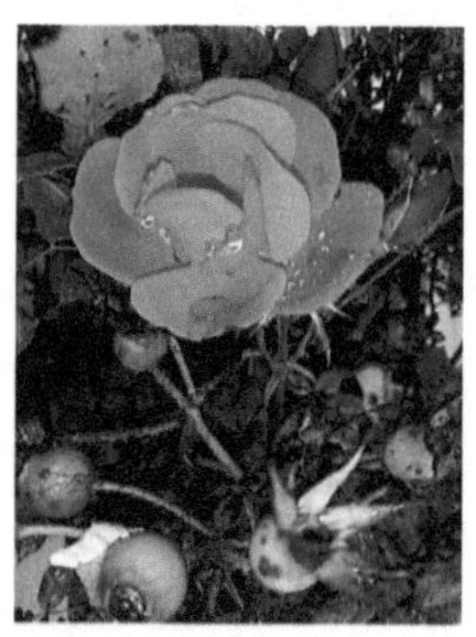

The longer I live,
The more I see,
Most, if not all, humans
are similar to me.
We each have gone through
At least one
Deep,

Dark,
Storyline.
Some may pretend the chapter never happened.
Some may appear as if the hurt has all been cured.
But this ink never completely fades.
This I know.
We are all flowers with thorns,
Most striving—
To move beyond our sharp edges.
Knowing that giving love,
And grace,
Is the only way
Into the light
For ourselves.

# A HEAVENLY MESSAGE

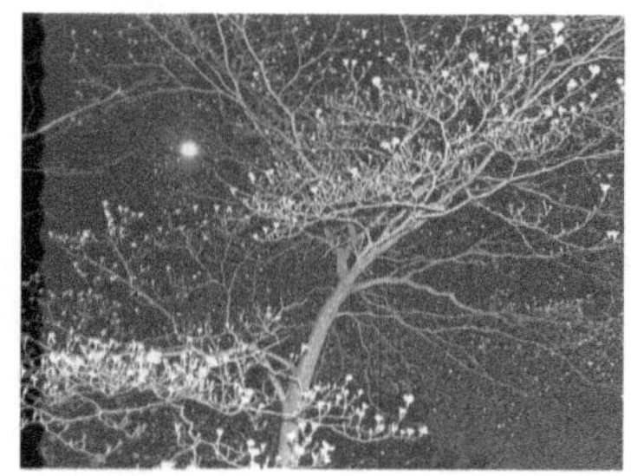

Branches
of lush green leaves,
like wands cast over me,
whispering an incantation through the wind,
*hope lives*.

# Three Syllables

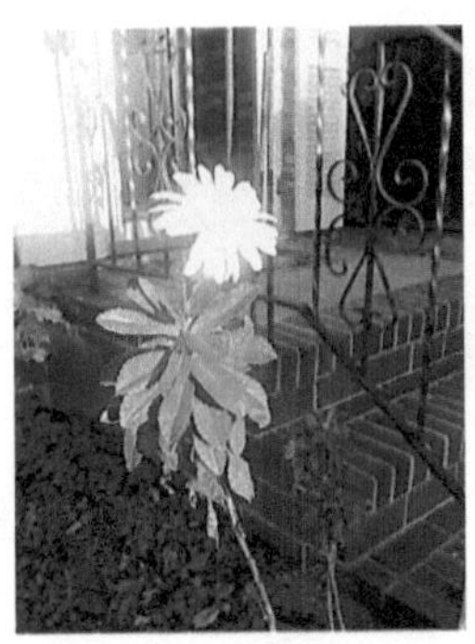

Your name in a burst of anger
Flew into my thoughts this morning.
I was heading out for a run,
But all I wanted to do was get on the phone with you.
There's no doubt my emotions come down to simply a
lot of missing you.

# Role Model

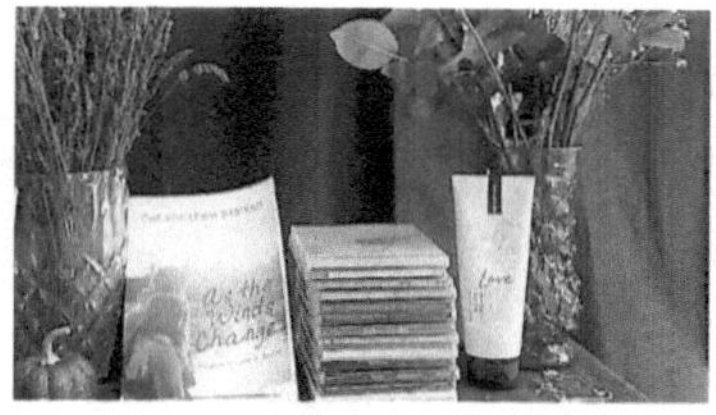

I thought you had your story all together,
but then I heard your songs on the radio.
I didn't think I'd still hear the angst in your voice.
I thought I would no longer be able to relate to you.
I was worried the soul would all be gone,
but there are still cries in your carried-out notes today,
some greater than before.
You have me moving, swaying, and singing along,
painting me a picture of a level of love I haven't yet
experienced,

but feel in the autumn winds.
I can imagine this sweet love,
and there is still the wanting.
I see this now.
There is still the need to create,
something only your soul can make.
Thank you.
Your gift taught me,
hearts like ours never stop.

# I Love You

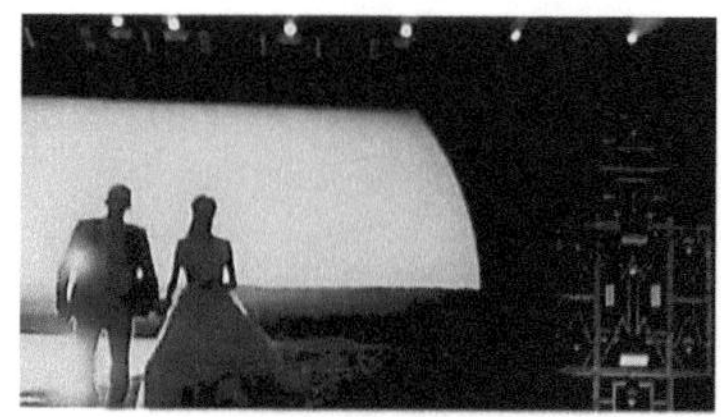

"I love you" is more than a goodnight phrase,
more than "you surprisingly captured my attention today,"
made me laugh harder than anyone else,
made me smile bigger than anyone else.
"I love you" is adoration in the ups and downs,
and every emotion in between.
I
Love

You,

for exactly who you are,

within every blessed minute we are given,

into our forever place, forevermore.

# SUMMER STORMS

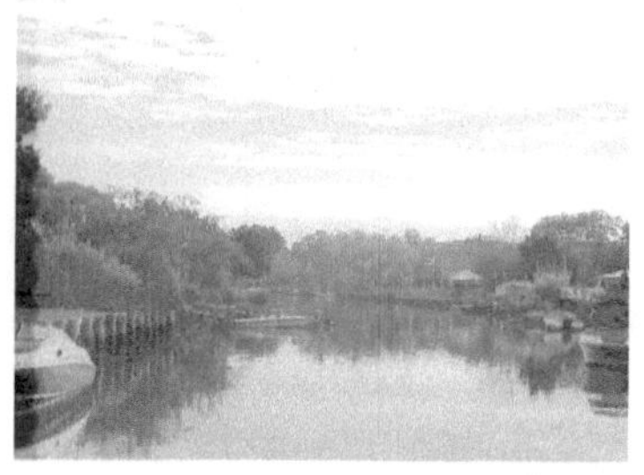

The faint light through forest green leaves,
crackling thunder,
has me anxious inside and out,
wanting to rush outside to you,
to laugh and dance in the warm-air rain
pouring down on the two of us.

# Sixteen Candles Lit

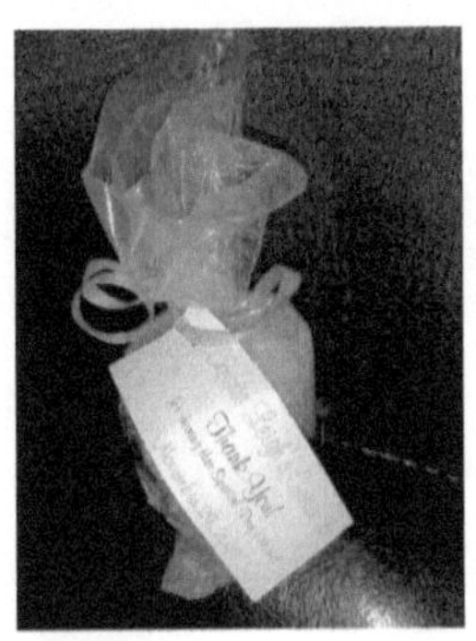

The dance stays with me,
Twirling slowly on darker days.
Around and around we go.
I didn't want to feel trapped in your arms.
I didn't want to feel flushed with disrespect,
to you and to myself.
I didn't want to still ache looking back.

I wanted to genuinely love you.
I wanted to feel like the luckiest girl in the world.
I wanted you to be my example.
I didn't want to ever feel such conviction when closing
off a piece of my heart,
but that is what happens every time I recall the dance.
Around and around we go in this memory,
I stop us every time and rip myself away,
Feeling the tears and swallowing them back
Every time.

# Seventeen Years Ago

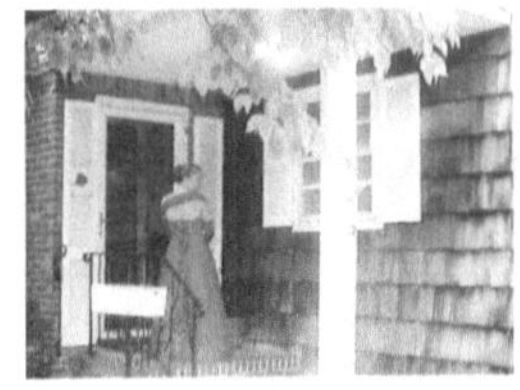

I look back

To this world of its own,

Through hundreds of self-present teenage eyes,

Talking about the future with fantastical perspectives,

Like we had much more than a clue.

Everything would be different once we graduated.

We were right about that.

To us, in that time, our lives were never so significant.

We knew, we never felt so much.

Our hearts beating like the marching band's drums,

In love, angst, and heartbreak,

As if everyone could hear,

As if an individual spotlight shined on each and every one of us.

In the midst of everyday changes,

Many of us dreamed of the final dance.

*Prom was that moment we would always look back on,*

We were told.

And for some, this was true as well.

For me, my memories are four years collectively,

Where passion had been set in front of me rather naturally.

It was then that I noticed within me a unique soul like never before,

A guide that walks beside me to this day,

A reminder that we are the embodiment of all our ages as we continue to grow.

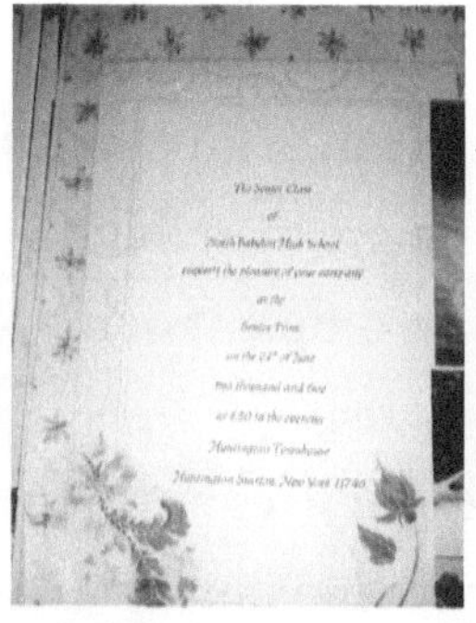

# STIRRED

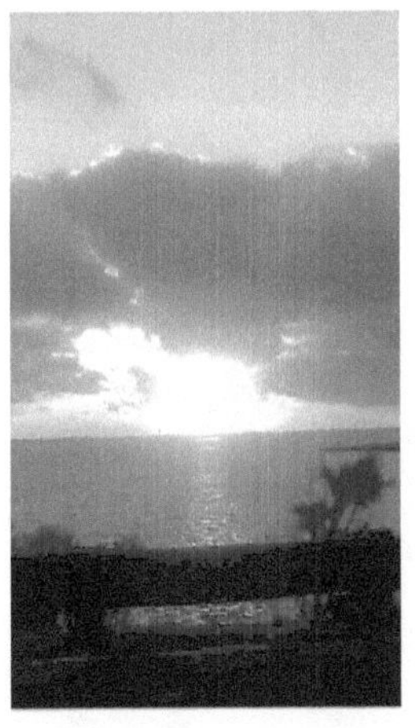

Ocean breeze-kissed night,

Ice Cream-colored sunset of lavender,

Orange,

And the softest blue,

Has me thinking about time

Stretching along,
With this same soul of mine,
Shifting,
Though I haven't known which way to go
For a long time now.
Drifting always in the way of my heart.
But it's been long since I've been bold,
It's been long since I've danced without thought.

# WRONG SIDE OF THE BED

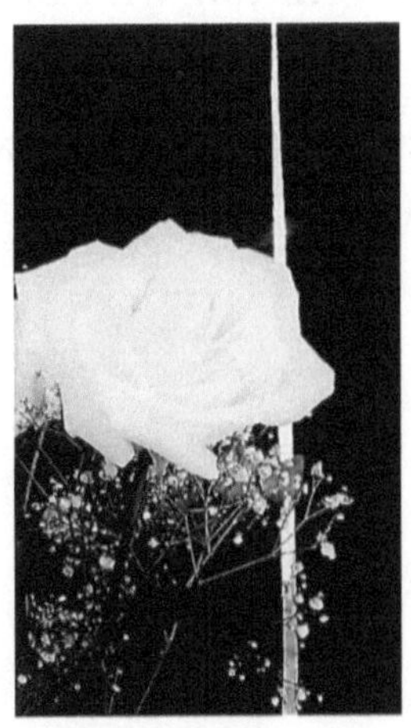

Light peeks through the opening of my dark blue
curtains.
My skin feels heavy,
as if my cheeks can still be flushed from the day before.
Every imperfection I believe I have,

I'm convinced everyone has taken notice.
I lay in my bed,
Eyes looking upward at the ceiling—
In need of repainting, too.
Caught in this irritatingly common human experience,
I turn over on my side to rest for a hopeful healing moment,
And that's when I finally begin to feel something different.
I feel grace.
I feel my view slowly shifting with all that is new calling to me,
Helping me slowly rise up from that wrong-side-of-the-bed perspective.

# BÉLA

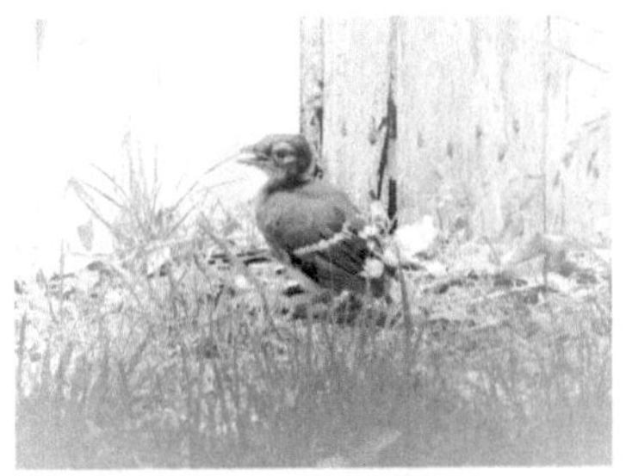

Baby Blue Béla touched ground today. Mama watched from the gate above. Dad watched from the treetop above the nest. Neither hovered, but they sang with each bold move their little one made. One parent would drop down every hour or so to nudge Béla before flying to a spot nearby. Béla would look up with his fuzzy little head in search of his parents, but they wouldn't make a peep. This was how they encouraged

their little one to be brave. This must have been diffi-
cult for them to do, but they believed in little Béla.

Every so often the parents would be sitting side by side
on the fence. I would surmise that similar to humans,
they needed the strength of each other at times. Baby
Blue Béla would flutter his wings, hop from dirt to the
low bark of a tree, and sometimes take a nap in the late
spring leaves. Mama would periodically drop down to
feed Béla, beak to beak, like kisses.

With determination and food in his tummy, Béla flew
higher and further each time he tried. Béla's eventual
flight came quicker than anyone could catch sight of.
And his parents we could later hear, singing out a
steady chirping of what sounded like joyful new begin-
nings. This was a process and first experience I am
blessed to have had with my own family at my side. Fly,
Béla, fly!

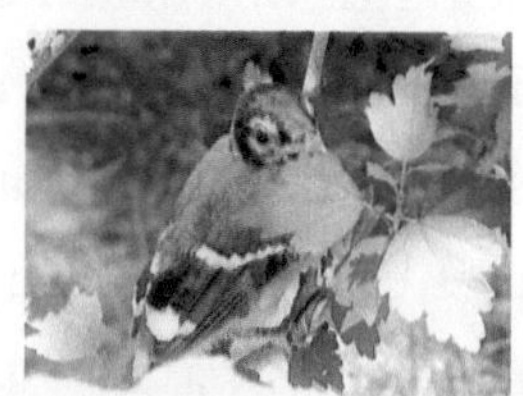

# Dream Chaser

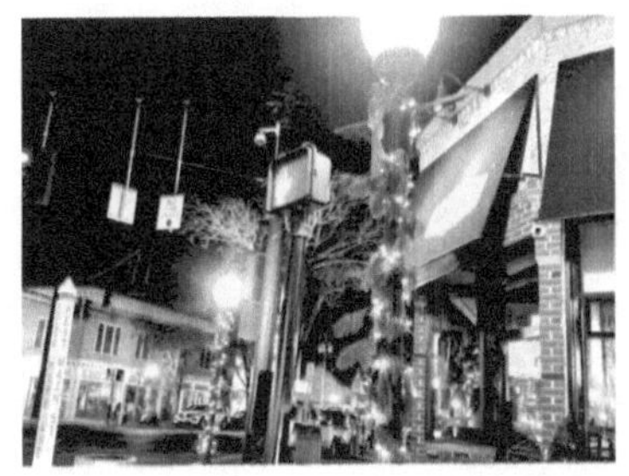

Who can you be if you never chase down a dream?
Even if you don't catch the wish,
Oh, the rich adventures to be had along the way,
All the twinkle-light-lit ones,
And the steel-gray downtown routes
you wouldn't have chosen if shown.
With after-sight in your pocket now,
You know you wouldn't change a line of this tale.

The drives of feeling alive with hope and identity,
On the rise to the top of your world,
Windows down,
Being unique,
Embracing exactly who you are.
When you went for a goal beyond your current status,
When you rebelled ever so slightly against the
embedded rules,
Oh, the way your spirit rose to the occasion each time!
When you were heartbroken but went out instead of
staying in,
When you experienced an unforgettable moment too
cherished to share,
Because you were brave,
Because your heart panged, and you listened this time.
It's the journey's stops that truly create our stories,
The beautiful life come true that you never thought to
dream of.

# In The Tree House

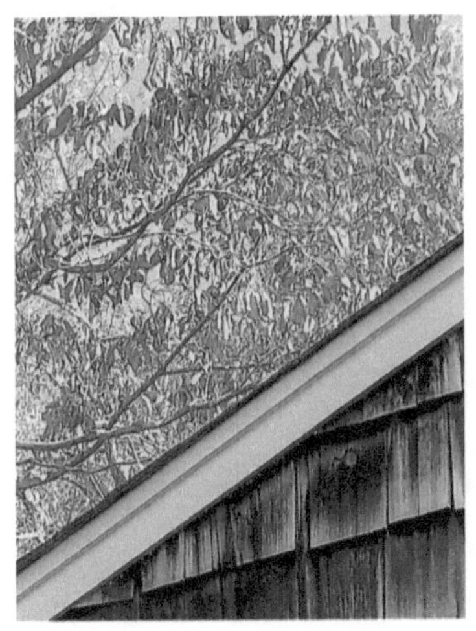

Way up high
In a tree house far away,
My stories wait for you,

Where I can see and not twist the tales
Out of perception fears,
Where your open arms wait for me to come on in.

# End of Spring

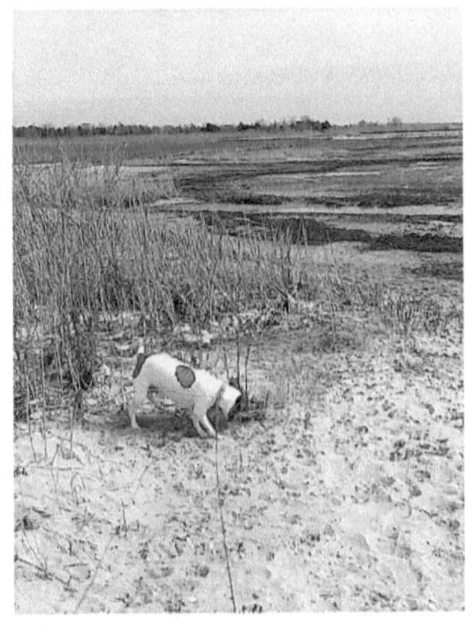

Angel wings white sunlight shines overhead.
A golden feeling of warmth covers my entire body.
A gentle, refreshing breeze extends

in ballet-like movement through my hair,
down to my bare feet dangling over the water.
My Jack Russell nudges me.
I am overcome with such faith-based possibility.

# THE ROMANCE OF SUMMER

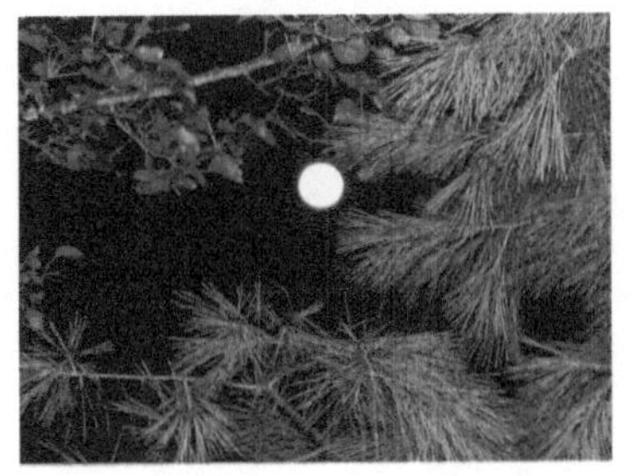

Wearing less clothing,
Being confident,
Feeling sexy,
No envy.
It's too hot to worry.
The day's sun beaming life upon me.
Steamy air,
Slower days,

Longer nights;
There are delicious excuses
To do much of what I want.
Flowers that did not bloom the year before,
Now showing buds
In the midnight firefly glowing garden,
Where I grow as well,
In the stillest, most romantic season of eternal youth.

# PICTURING YOU

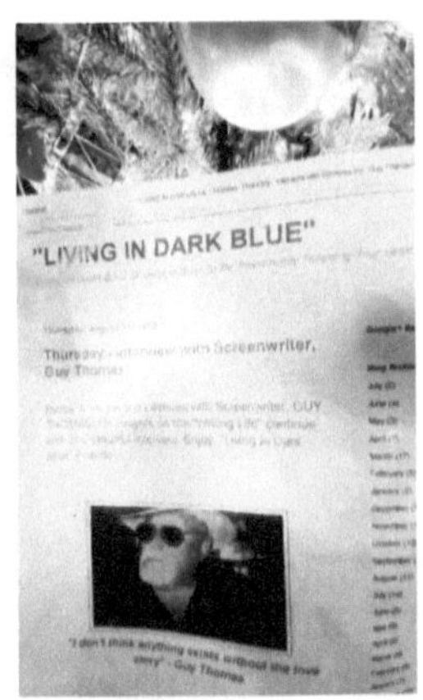

You ride horseback into my mind almost every day,
Yet you don't seem to send a single wave my way.
I feel these may really be the end times,
Without you being in this world.
A dreamer for all sixty-six of your years,

Off to Heaven, I am sure you went the same way.

I imagine the ground must have shaken a little when

you arrived,

Inventing stories the moment your spirit landed,

I'm sure Heaven is a bit different these days.

Coming in like Bonaparte,

My grandparents playing parts in every script you start.

Well, not Grandma,

Another bold spirit not content to simply rest

Or follow what another thinks is best.

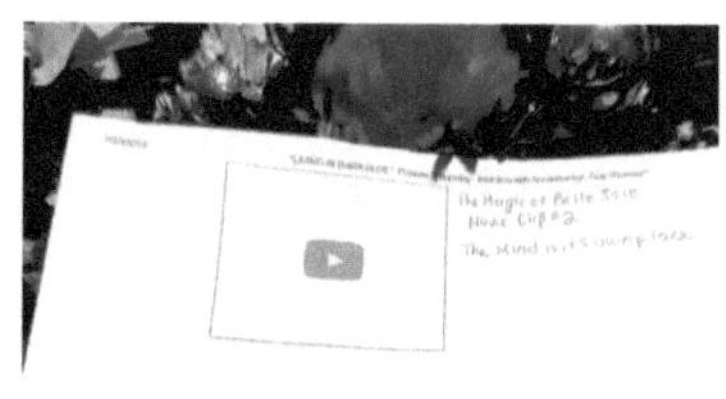

Interview with Screenwriter, Guy Thomas:

CL: Writing, I believe, causes one to develop and change constantly as a human being with the creation of a work. What are some new ideas you may have acquired in your writing life?

GT: The main thing is sometimes individuals come into your life unexpectedly, and they are the catalysts for change. Also, the environment you put yourself in changes you. I believe places and individuals are the sources that change your work, and in turn cause you to develop as a human being and writer.

# Toxic Belief

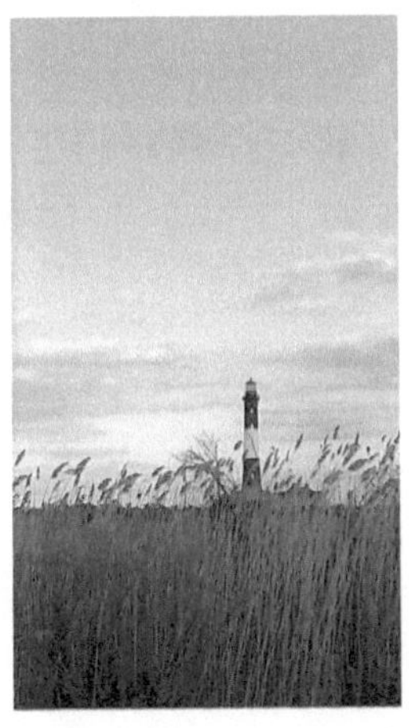

She takes the high road away,
Leaving traces of ragweed in her tracks.
Further and further, she goes,
Until you can no longer follow.

Your opinions of her rising up into the archives of her
mind,
Never to go away but to carry less presence as time
goes on.
There's a passed-down temperament you seem to have
claimed.
There's a belief that all men are above all women,
Our ultimate purpose to serve and bear,
You sadly viewed her this way.
You tried to break her down.
*She really thinks she's something, doesn't she?*
*"A lot of nerve," you would say.*
You didn't like how she never conformed.
But, she is the same one you once encouraged.
You used to cheer her on,
When she was a child—
The same being with the golden arm,
And fearless dives she made into the powerful Atlantic
waves.
Now, she is using the bravery you once admired
on you.
She is walking away.
It's too bad you'll never get to be a part of how high
she will fly.

# OTHER WORLD

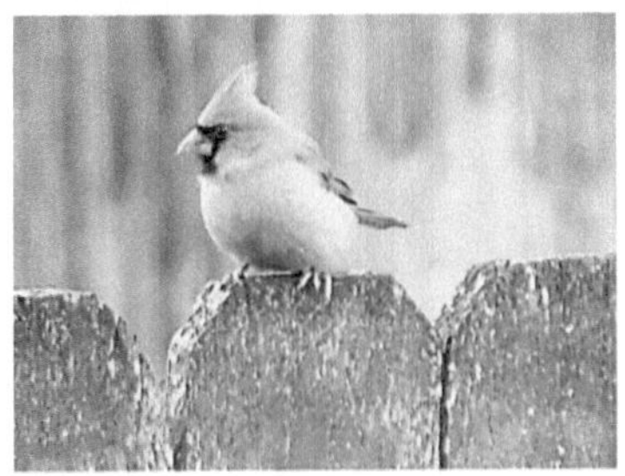

You'll probably never know the space you took up in
my heart.
You regularly sound in my thoughts,
A message of endings to the tune of the Mourning
Dove
On a rainy morning.
While I still fly in like the bright red Cardinal

For a moment each week,
Quiet,
Waiting to see if you'll come to join me,
But you are content to stay in this other world it seems.

# Crystal Clear Wisdom

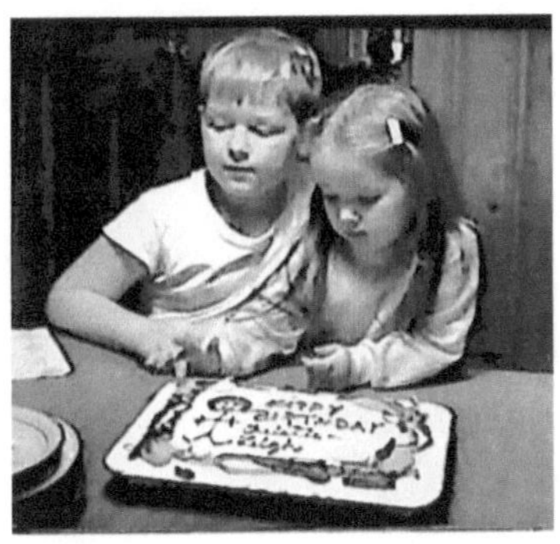

What would you say?
What would you do?
I conclude there must be a reason we each live in the
time we do.
One truth though, I know you would tell—
We must go,

To where the kindred spirits continue to harvest
vibrant and rich fruit,
And tell fireside stories of legends and love.
You would direct us toward where our hearts have
been pulling us all along.

# Aid to Patience

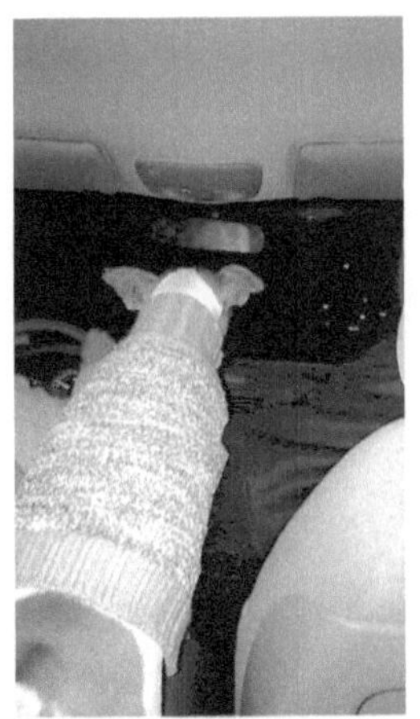

Patience:

The answer is gratitude.

To recall the chocolate-dipped moments,

And sunset-lit blessings of genuine love and adventure.

That is what sets us free as we wait for each and
every key.

# SEPTEMBER EVE

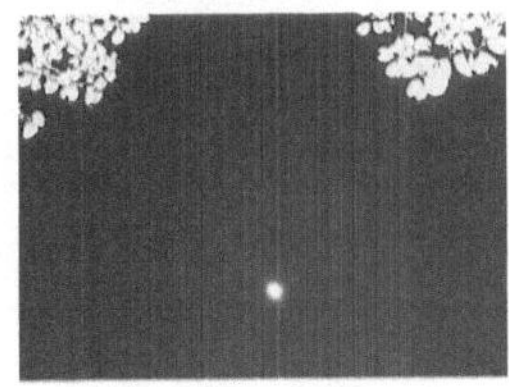

There's such change in the air.
I gaze out at the dimming blue sky
Through thick forest leaves on the trees.
I rest in a late summer stillness with blind anticipation,
As crickets chirp,
On this departure night from the blazing August heat.
Refreshing winds swim unseen,
This September Eve,
And I look forward to my calendar's blank spaces.

Blessed but dreaming.
Letting go but holding on.
Fearful but excited.
I am intrigued by storylines yet to be revealed,
This September Eve.

# Under the Influence

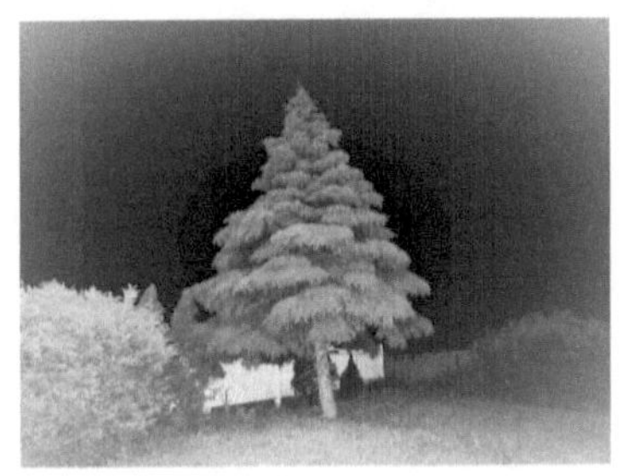

At our start,
We are blind beings,
Hearts open,
Set to trust,
Bearing our souls to traitors,
To rebuild with walls.

# October Passion

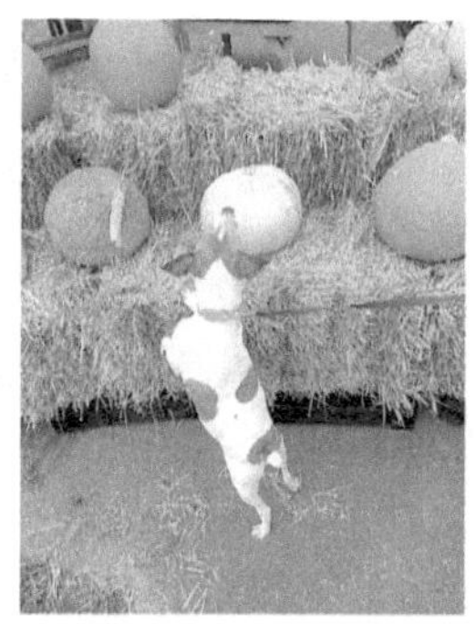

October sky night,
Soul-lit faith,
Fall breeze sparks magic.

# TO A PEARL

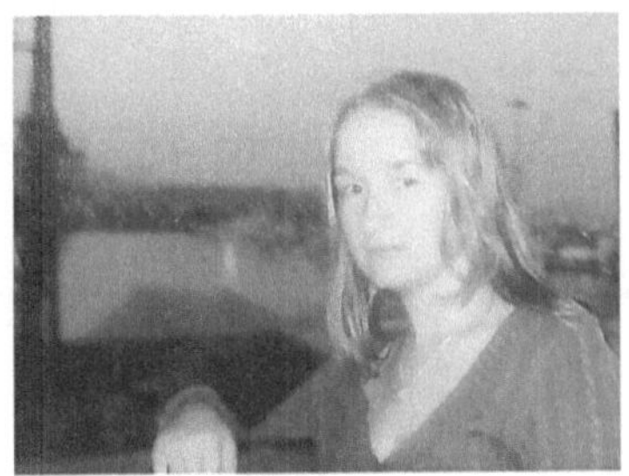

If I could tell twenty-year-old me what I know now,
I'd say to stop putting stock in what others say.
Don't lock your mind up in highlighted tales.
This life is not a straight path for anyone.

So run cold water over your face.
Pick yourself up girl, stand up straight.
You've got magic in your veins.

Find what sparks the opening to your garden gate.

If I could tell twenty-year-old me what I know now,
I'd tell her to play the songs that negate all negativity.
Fill your soul constantly with recollections of genuine
love.
'Cause, no one can ever change your vision of light
but you.

So run cold water over your face.
Pick yourself up girl, stand up straight.
You've got magic in your veins.
Find what sparks the opening to your garden gate.
And walk on in.

# A Haiku on You

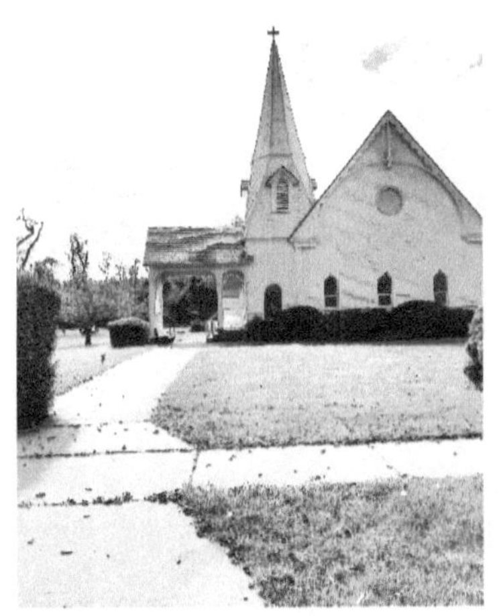

You declare your faith.
You wrap yourself in the flag.
But hurt everyone.

# COMMON MASK

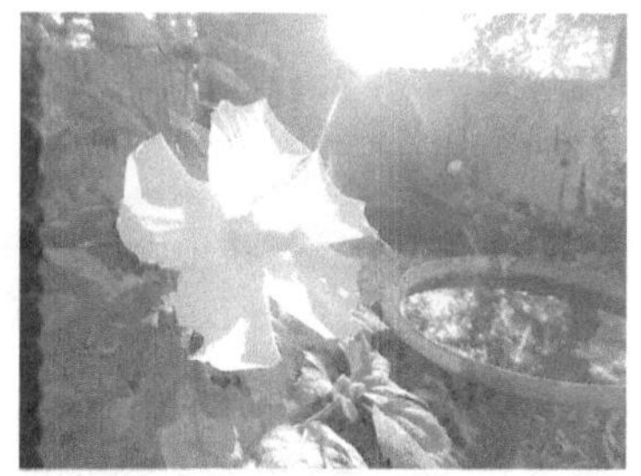

Religion,
You use as a shield.
Etiquette,
You have none.
Running on self-righteousness,
You are not holy.

# Don't Even Skip
# A Beat

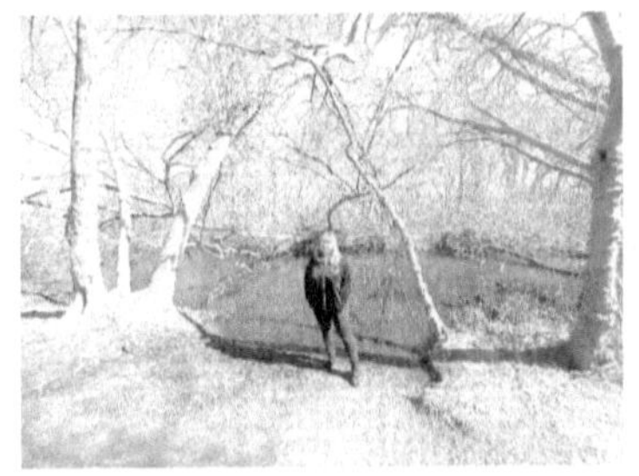

Don't even skip a beat, girl.
He didn't value the pearl that you are.
Don't wait to catch the next train,
Your heart deserves so much more.
Don't waste thoughts on loneliness,
Within you, there is a sparkling rainbow of power.
He was not a companion,
You must know by now.

Lost in his immediate wants and desires,
His heart was never open for you.
So please do not even skip a beat, girl,
There are incredible people and places waiting—
To come in once you have cleared your soul of his
space.

# Hypocrite

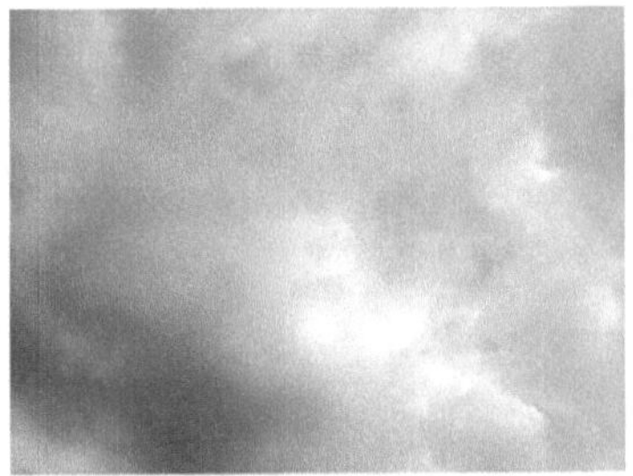

You declare your faith,
Hiding truth.
Toxic to your core.

# A Man (To Me)

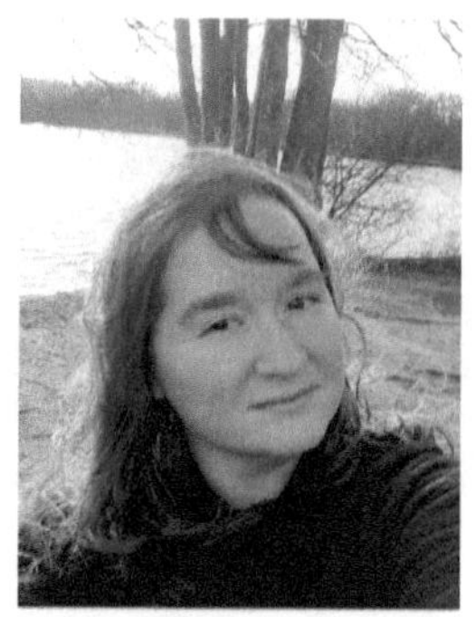

A man drives if she asks him to.
Knows when to push,
And when to step back.
But he always comes back
With nothing but the deepest love.
He wants to know her story.

He asks questions out of genuine interest.
He makes her feel bigger in beauty and natural ability,
Not smaller.
He holds her tight when she needs him the most,
And respects her boundaries.
He knows the difference between being encouraging,
And disrespecting her fears.
A man, to me, listens.
And when he doesn't understand,
He gives her the space until he can.
He processes the ache between her words,
And never comes from a judgment space
Because he cares for her.
He wants and needs for her to feel safe.
Ulterior desires are not in a back pocket of tricks.
He would never try to manipulate her,
Thinking he knows better.
He doesn't ever define her by past traumas she
may own.
He values every kink in her armor,
Seeing nothing but remarkable strength and heart.
He trusts her knowledge and instincts.
And this real good man in turn,
He receives more than he could have imagined—
A profound and everlasting love.

He is overwhelmed in the best way
With love,
Unwavering gratitude,
And sacred preciousness,
More than he could have ever imagined,
Every single day.

# Chasing Sunsets and Wishing on Cardinals

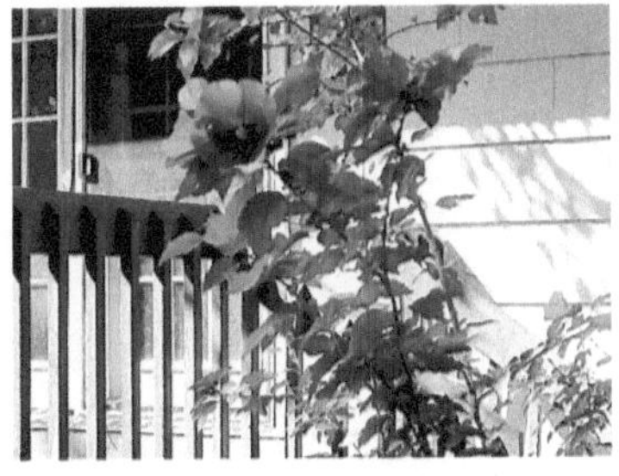

Yesterday, I stood beneath an orange and pink sky.

For days, the bold red birds fluttered fast past my eyes.

I'd grab my camera every time,

Only to capture the blur of color,

In sunsets and the Cardinals' chirps of goodbye.

But yesterday, I stood beneath an orange and pink sky.

I heard a Cardinal sing loudly from the rooftop of my

house,

And I watched as this little bird stayed.

With no camera in hand,

I looked up at the sunset too,

And it was then that I realized,

With the wind ushering in an overwhelming sense of

peace,

Some miracles and signs are not meant to be captured.

Some moments are meant to be held onto by the

heart's memory alone.

# Forever Entwined

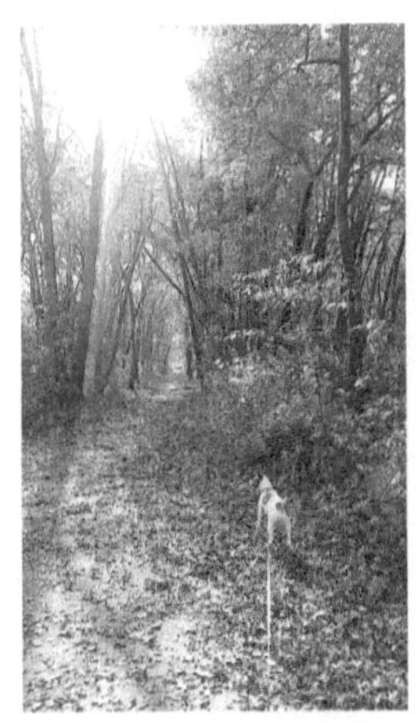

You've stayed on my mind,
Like autumn, golden reed-lined boardwalk hikes,
And crisp northeast winds welcoming my kind,
The ones who turn away from the masses' likes.

You've stayed with me because you've understood me,
Like my favorite light blue knit sweater,
Hugging me in your warmth when I've lost all hope
to see,
Reminding me that my bright spirit can transform any
weather.

You've stayed on my mind,
A spirit that does not hide.
We will forever be entwined,
Even if it is only in my memory that you reside.

# Unsaid

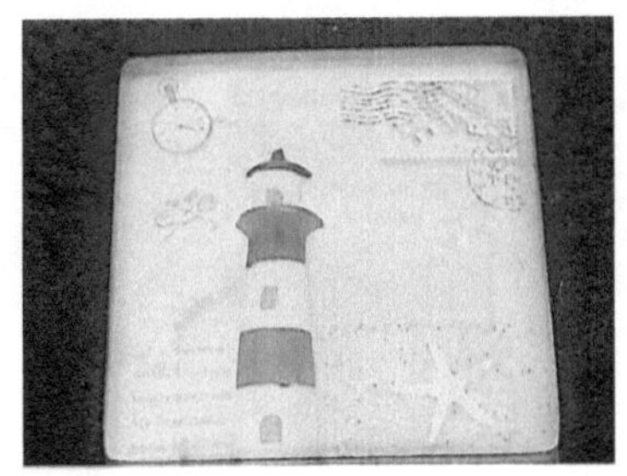

All these homes,
All these different stories,
Through dimly lit windows,
This autumn night.
And I wonder...
What is to come,
Of all the feelings we push down?
All that we distract ourselves with,

To stop ourselves from expressing,
The many thoughts that have become politically and
socially incorrect to say,
All that could potentially save our conscience-empty
world?

# THE DREAM

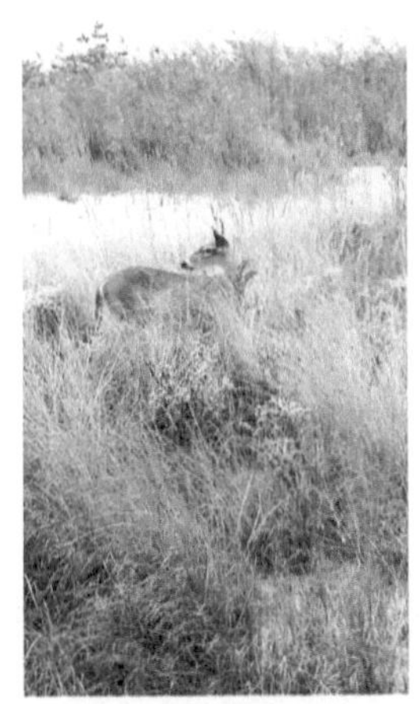

To run away
With only my immediate family
And all the animals of the world,
Set free,

To a place where the brainwashed humans cannot
reach.
An unspoken spirit will be the only key,
Communicating through souls,
The way Heaven is said to be.
To live in an endless land,
Filled with wildflowers and unwavering love,
That is the dream.

# For A Healthy Soul

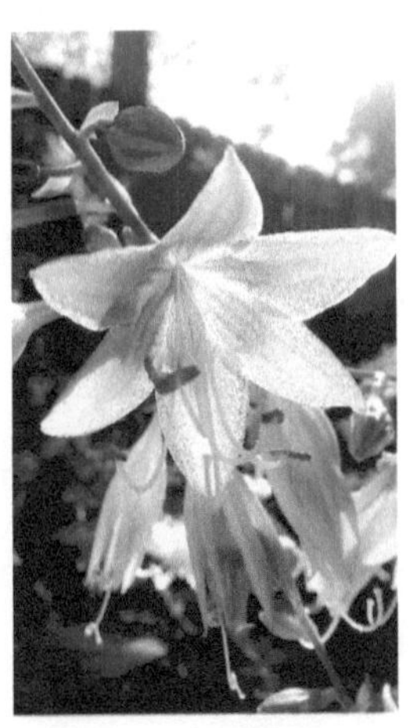

She needs to remind herself from time to time,
Sometimes hour to hour,
She is in control of what she says yes to.
When the cold water pours down on her from the
showerhead above,

Or she runs until her thighs burn from the release of
every ounce of energy,
It's then that she instinctively knows,
Right on the beat,
Her answer,
Her truth.
She needs to remind herself to take the time
sometimes,
Put in the effort or give in to the release,
But always know,
She is in absolute control of what she says yes to,
and when it's *absolutely no.*

# MY JACK, ALISTAIR

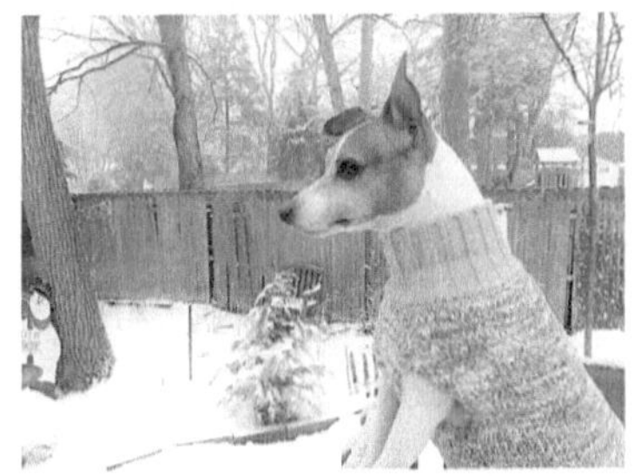

A boy who overwhelms my heart every day.
Leaping into each morning, he is my greatest teacher.
Irreplaceable, he has left forever pawprints on my soul.
Stylish from his personality to the sweaters he wears.
Taking center stage at night with the toss the treat
game he plays.
A won't put up with any distractions, smart little guy.

Impish when he knows that you know exactly what he
wants.
Revealing a thousand expressions of love every day,
that is my Alistair.

# CHE SUZ

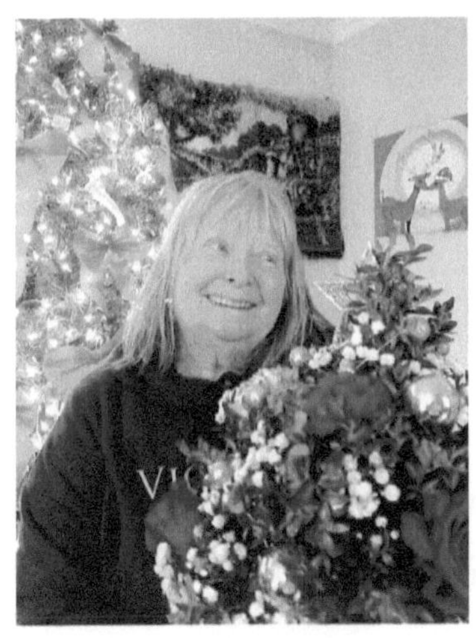

Coming up with your own nickname, it's quintessentially you.
Heart on your sleeve but mischief on your mind,

Eloise at the plaza would be your cartoon counterpart.
Star at your core.
Un-matched in your creativity.
Zealously perfect in your sense of devotion, love, and
child-like wonder.

# Faith

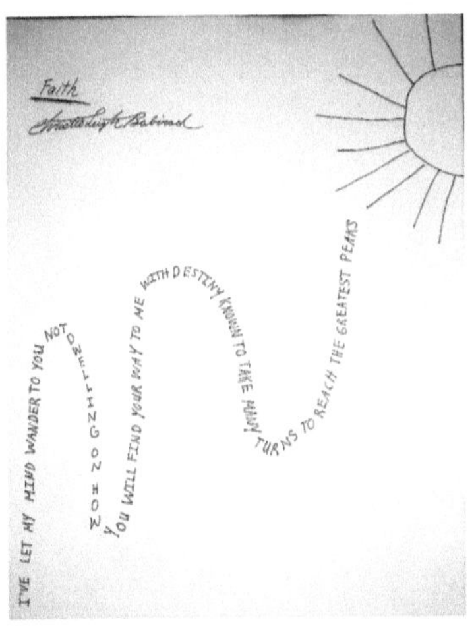



I've let my mind wander to you,
Not dwelling on how
You will find your way to me,

With destiny known to take many turns
To reach the greatest peaks.

# IMMERSED IN A MEMORY

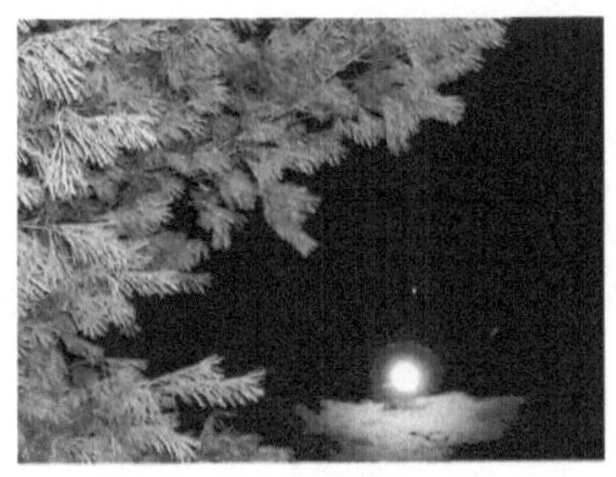

Immersed in memory of early fall evenings,
Parked by the sidewalk curb on a storefront street,
Was the scent of fried rice,
Wafting in through the window of my passenger seat.
A whistle sounded from the high school further down
the avenue,
Loud cheering,

Crickets continuing to chirp deeper into the night,
Cars whooshing by,
The feel of crisp winds trailing through my hair,
And adrenaline in my heart—
Thinking about tomorrow.

# ROBBIE

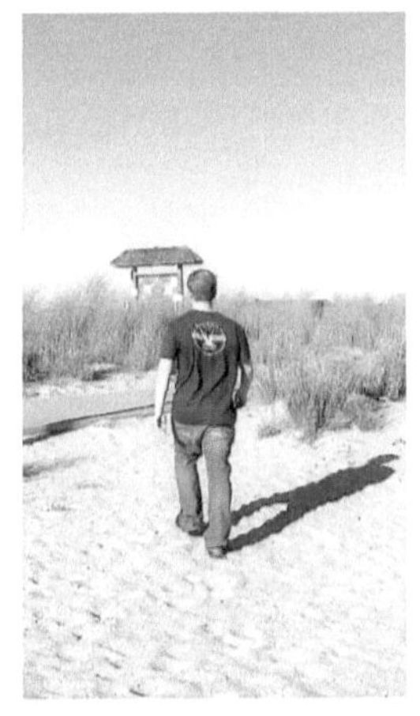

Renegade of creative expansion.
Open thinker,
Builder of the never seen before.
Box? There is no box.

Intelligent listener.
Enigmatic to surface-level folks.

# STILL WITH US

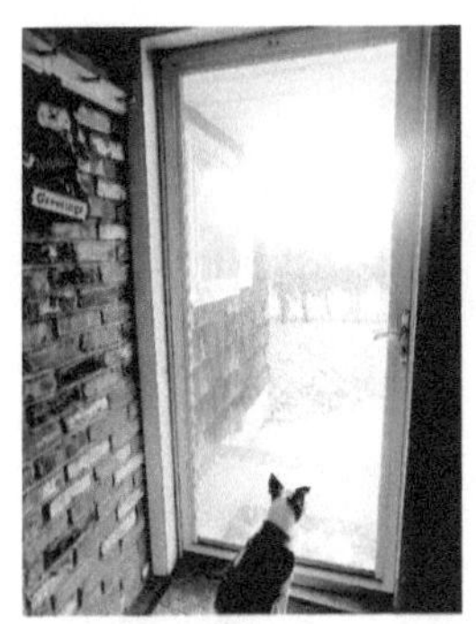

Spirits,
Halloween night,
Stroll past Trick O' Treaters,
Through front doors to visit family,
Content.

# A Symbol

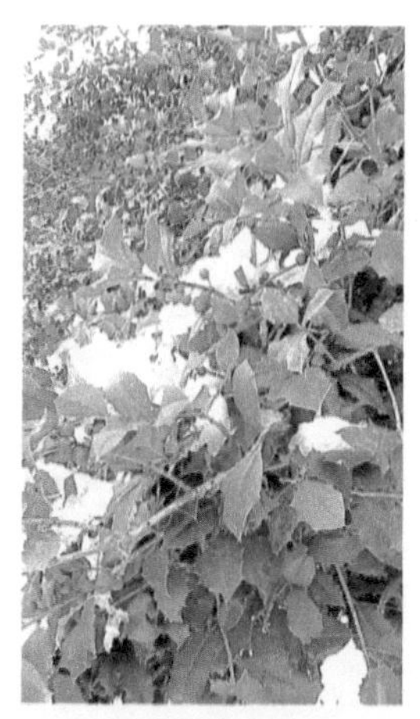

Berries,
Of Holly leaves,
Bright ruby-red kisses,
Glistening on sunlit lime leaves,
Blossom.

# The Viewer

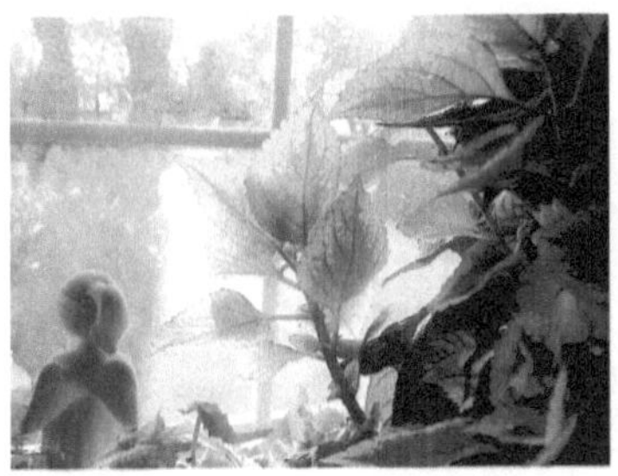

The viewer has the choice to see with both the eyes and
heart,
But without vision, won't reach far beyond its start.

# ONE STEP

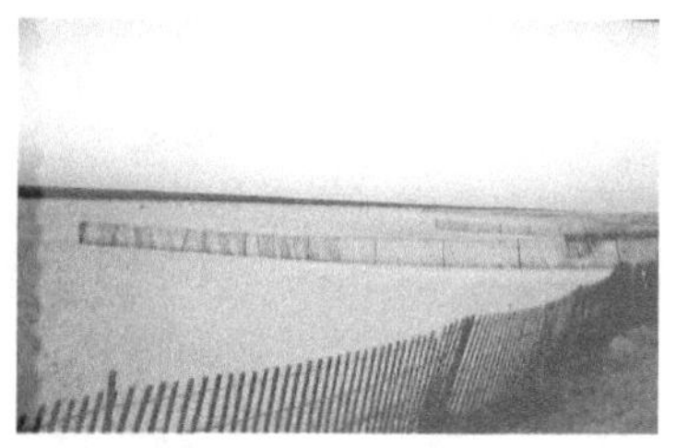

Take one step,
Toward your newest dream.
And listen.
Do you hear?
The rush of new beginnings,
Like waves on the sea.

# MY FIX

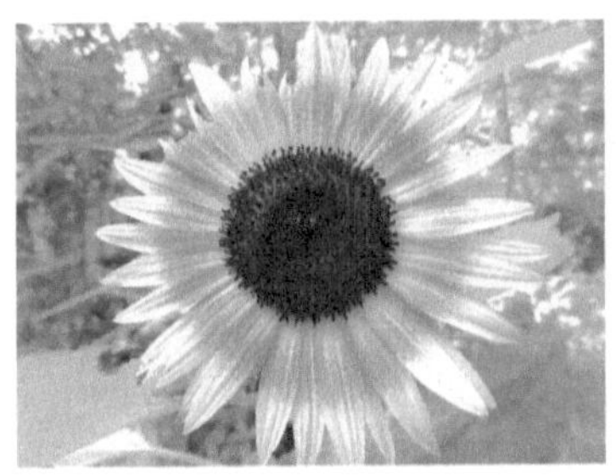

Country Love Songs
Bring me home,
With a grounded-in-substance embrace
From those who know how to hold on just right,
Fitting into my soul naturally,
Closing in those broken spaces,
Taking me high and fast,
To open places.

# My Choice

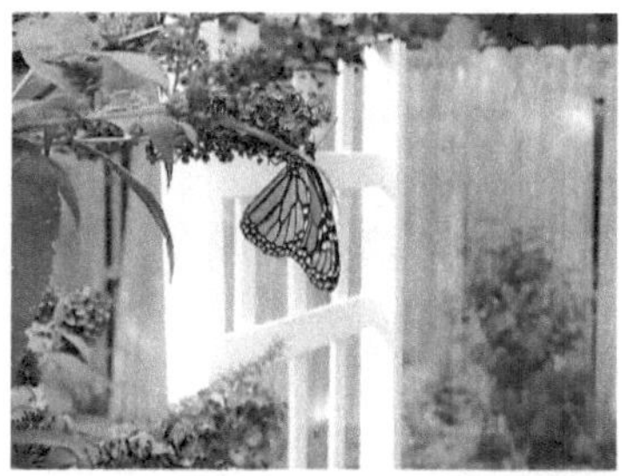

These are tragic times we live in,
Where most can rationalize the worst of crimes.
But these are also extraordinary times,
Where one has many channels to express themself,
Where your wildest dreams can in fact come true,
With determination and creativity.
And I choose to dwell on this side of the coin,

Where I rush to take a picture
Of the sunrise orange and black Monarch Butterfly,
That landed on my shoulder.
This butterfly was sent to tell me,
"Everything is going to be okay."

# ONLY LOVE REMAINS

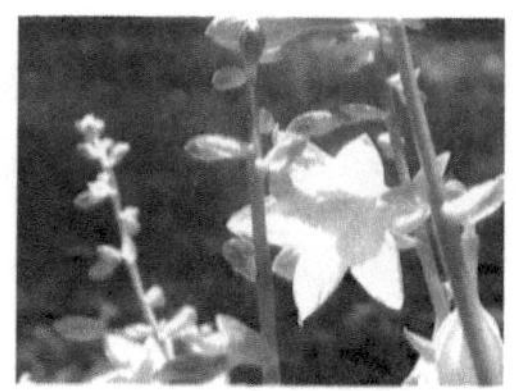

I don't miss the fighting I felt would never end.
Yet somehow, when your spirit rose up,
Much of my resentment died with your earthly frame.
Now, I reflect on how you showed up for my every
event,
This big smile of pride on your face;
"Here's my picture, so you won't forget me," you said.
How could I forget you?
And even you, with your impish smile and creative
determination.

It seems at the end of the story,
For me at least,
It is only love I have for the two of you.
Everything else has fallen away.

# As Thanksgiving Nears

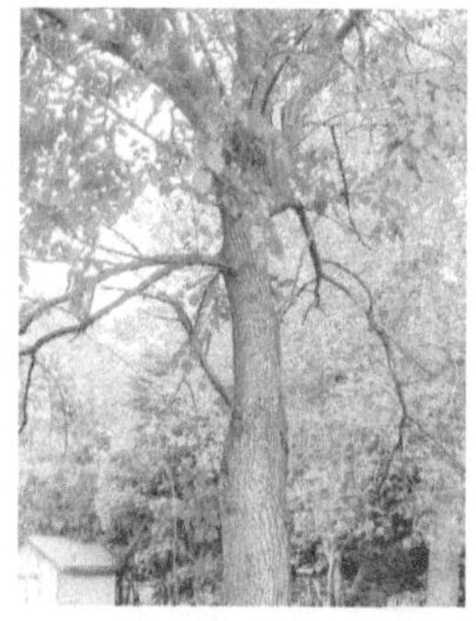

Excitement rides on the crisp winds.

The days become bold with plans and events.

Worries and static hours are replaced with youthful
hope.

The most genuine and true belief is stirred.

Purpose creeps into the weeks.

The heart fills up with great creativity.

Trees steadily shed colorful leaves,
Falling poetically,
A tapestry is created of orange, yellow, and red
On a canvas of pavement, dirt, grass, and sometimes
sand.
Crunching is the sound,
Of boots and paws shuffling through wooded trails
All leading to the sparkling bay.
The blue sky becomes more vivid with each day.
And my mind wanders more and more
To the early morning sunrise,
A bounty of plated food on a gold tablecloth,
Crimson and orange flowers,
The living room set up for the parade,
Anticipation building for Santa coming in on the float,
Signaling the Christmas season is on its way.

# SIREN CALL

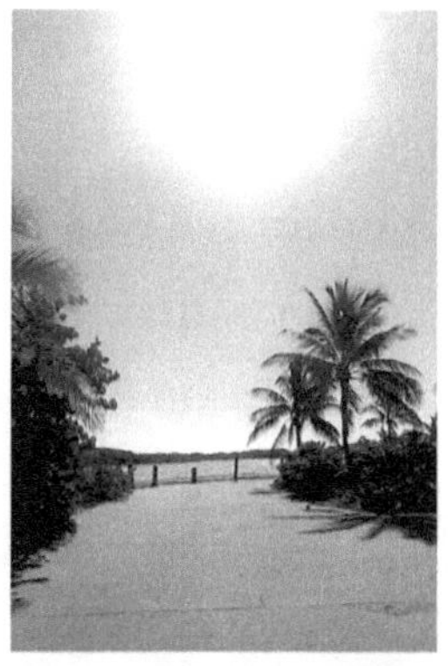

I've been talking with someone who makes me smile.
He doesn't play a single heart game
And does not desire any outward fame.
His attention toward me does not waver.
I have a feeling it's a love I could forever savor.

I'm about to fall for someone.
And this is my call out to you.
If you have any doubts,
If you remember the feel of my lips on yours,
If I still linger brightly on your mind,
Reach out to me.

I still think about you.
The way you loved me, still lingers brightly on my
mind,
And I remember the feel of your lips,
So smooth and right.

But I'm about to fall for someone new.
This is my siren call out to you.
If you have any doubts,
If you remember too—
The feel of my lips on yours,
If I still linger brightly on your mind,
Reach out to me.

# TWENTY TWENTY

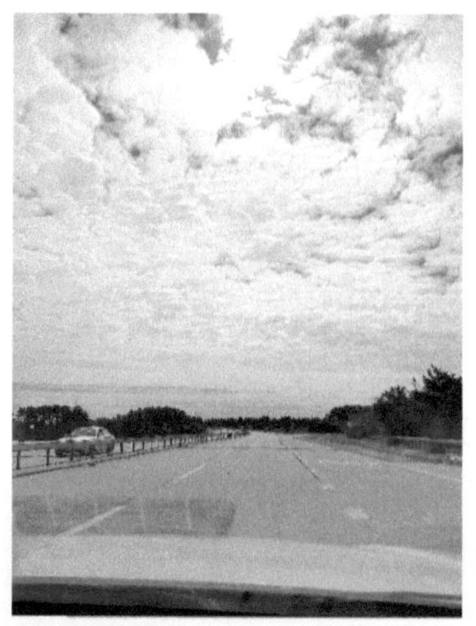

Twenty-twenty she fully became,
Now publicly moving down a middle lane.
Her strong beliefs would now be kept under lock
and key.

Consistencies in human nature she could finally see.

She grins at those who think society is more advanced.
All the future is learning to do is push buttons fast.
They proudly declare that they do not read.
They subscribe to whatever popular media seeds.
The world is no different than the days of beheadings.
Casting out souls different than the masses,
Done only today with more varied methods of control.

Yes, it was twenty-twenty that she fully became,
Traveling publicly down the middle lane.
Comprehending now,
Keeping few close will be how her life's fruits will gain.

# HELPLESS

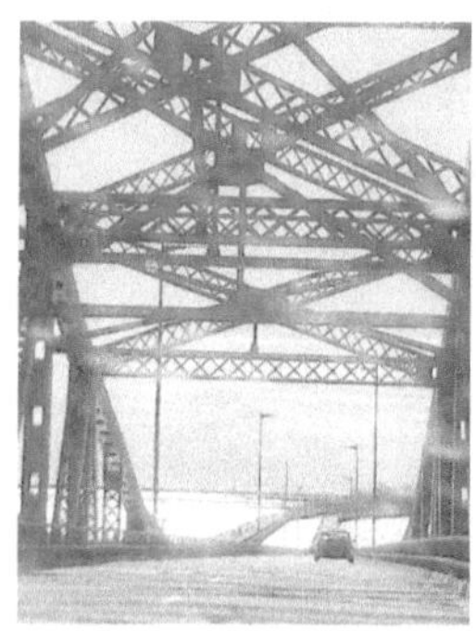

If only you could spend a day in my heart,
Aching to find a way to break through
The blockages in your mind
That have you furious with helplessness.
I know how and why you feel the way you do.
But a change desperately needs to come.
Only you can make the move,

When nothing I say or do will permanently fix you.
But maybe if you could spend a day in my aching
heart,
You would feel how profoundly I care for you,
How truly loved you are.

# FLAWED

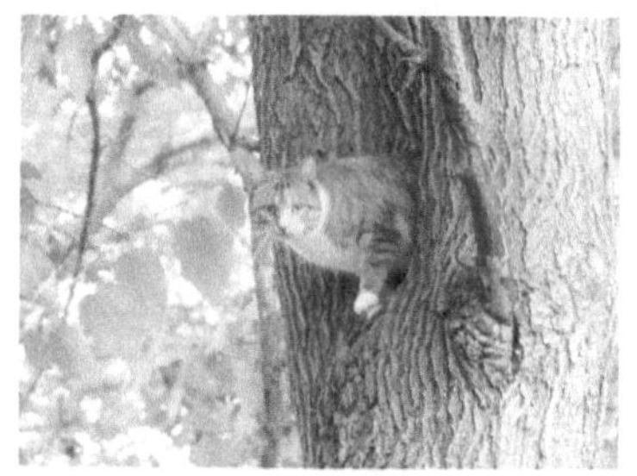

She is flawed.
Sensitive to touch.
Rash when hurt,
Insecure.
The cat on the hot tin roof.
Loves like no other.

# SOMEONE TO LISTEN
# TO ME

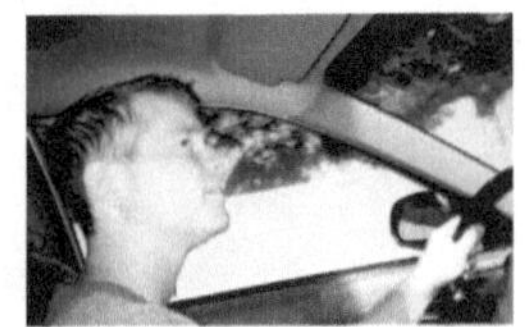

I was loud this morning,
talking about this and that.
You added to what I said.
You nodded your head.
In the moment you stayed,
not going somewhere else in your mind.
And when I was done;
I felt the tension leave my body.
I felt respected.
My voice has always been valued by you.

And I thought about how precious this is,
since I know the opposite better.
I know the restrained,
tears-choked-back hurt,
never experienced with you.

# Puzzle Pieces

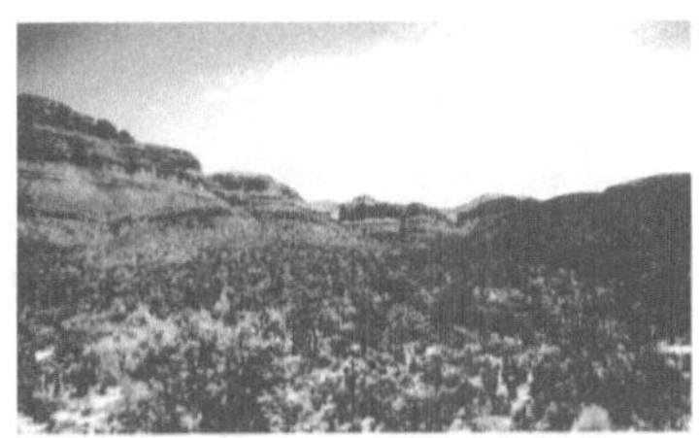

I see you in January,
Standing under a creamy pink sunset surrounded by
the Joshua trees.
I see me through your gaze,
Beautiful and free in a flowing, golden-flecked white
dress.

# At Home With You

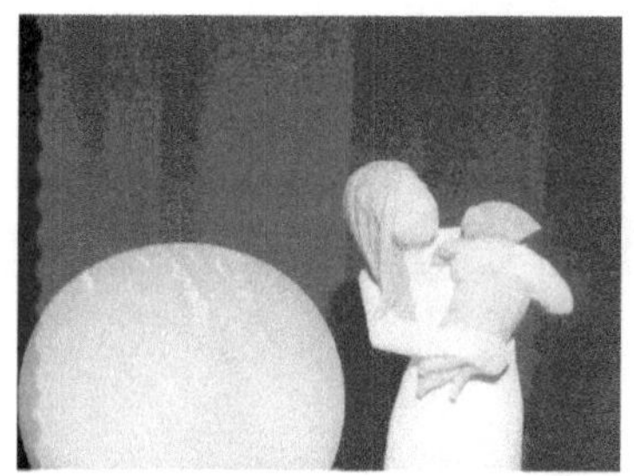

For most of my days,
All that I desire—
It's you and me,
Our Jack Russell,
In a cozy yellow-bulbed room filled with books,
Piano music playing softly on the stereo,
And rain falling down outside our windowpanes.

# Sweet Contradictions

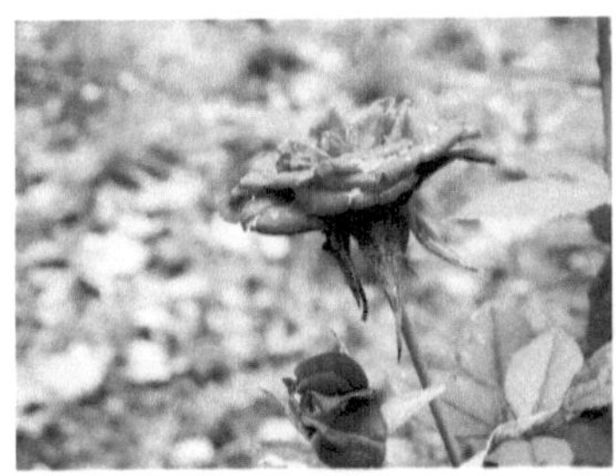

There's such a melancholy to joyous times,
But a sweetness in goodbyes,
Revealing that you have never loved more,
You have never felt more content,
That the magnificent will always triumph over the
darkness.
And these memories when held onto,
Bring a promise of much more to come.

# Island Girl Calling Me Home

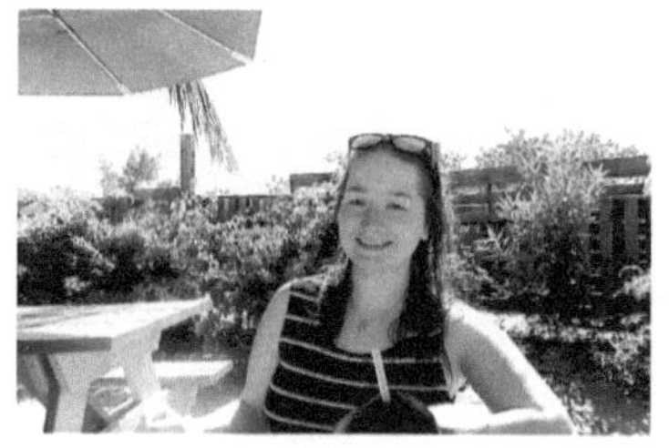

Let's sail away,
To the sun-soaked island in the tropics,
Where the air is carefree.
Maybe if I had never been here,
I wouldn't need this place so.
But now I know.
This is the destination that will open my constricted soul.

I can already smell the scent of steamed rice and baked
pastries
Under umbrella shade.
I can feel the warm breezes coming in off the
Caribbean Sea.
I'm ready to jump into those bright blue waters,
And lay on back.
I can hear the Calypso music,
And see the girl I never got to fully explore,
Dancing with her mom beside the band,
Barefooted—
An Island Girl.
She's calling me home.
There's an Island Girl inside of me.
Someone I could forever be.
She's still a large part of me.

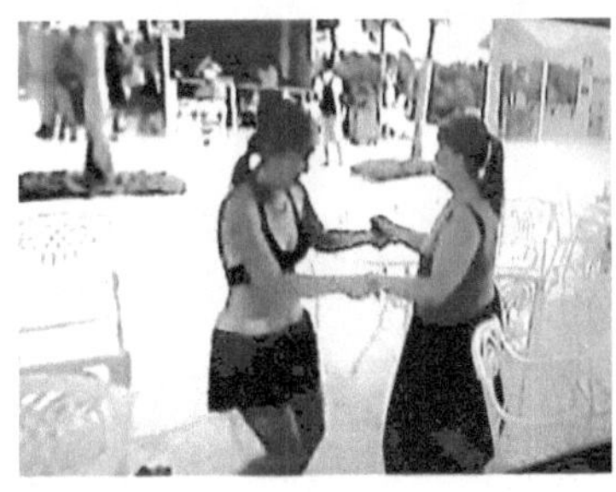

# My Queen, My Mother

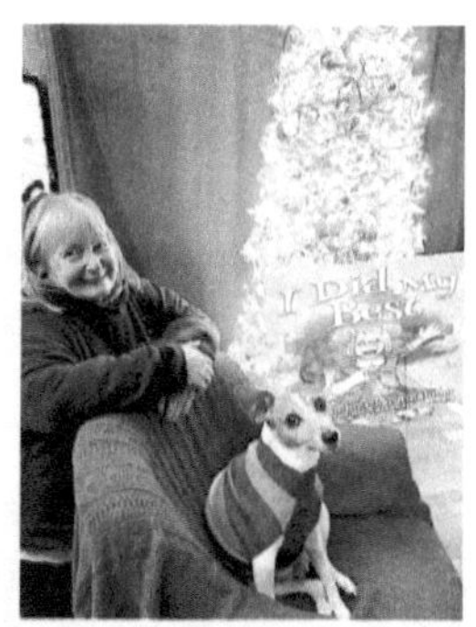

She keeps life magical,
Believing
in that golden, sparkling light
from the ancient, overlooked wooden storage chest,
that can always be found,
no matter the corner of life I find myself in.

She is the one who keeps the soundtrack playing in my
heart,
All the Disney and Broadway stories
of finding my way through the dark and tangled woods
of loud, unfamiliar, scary sounds,
of trees rustling in the wind
and owl cries through the night.
She reminds me that there will always be friends too,
if I open my heart,
no matter the corner of life I find myself in,
no matter how dreary the chapter or scene may seem.
With her, the music always plays me out into the
assurance,
I will receive everything and more that I have
dreamed of.

# THE PRAYER

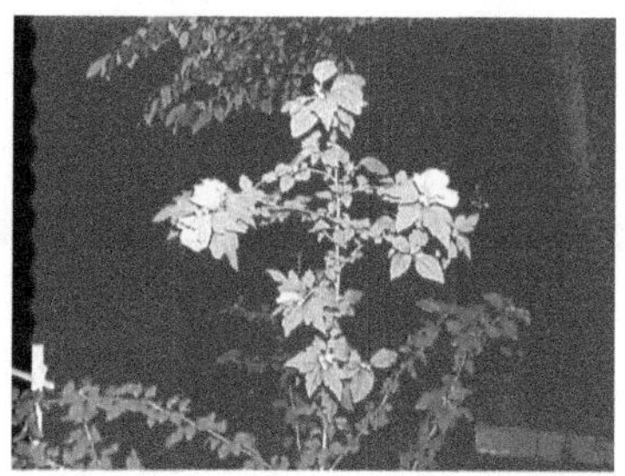

Do you remember when we sang "The Prayer"? Have you heard the song since our time? The melody still brings tears to my eyes and instantly I am wrapped in the blanket you used to be. I wonder if you still recall the softness between you and me, and if you sometimes long to jump back when this world feels worse by the day, like I do.

# That Early November Feeling

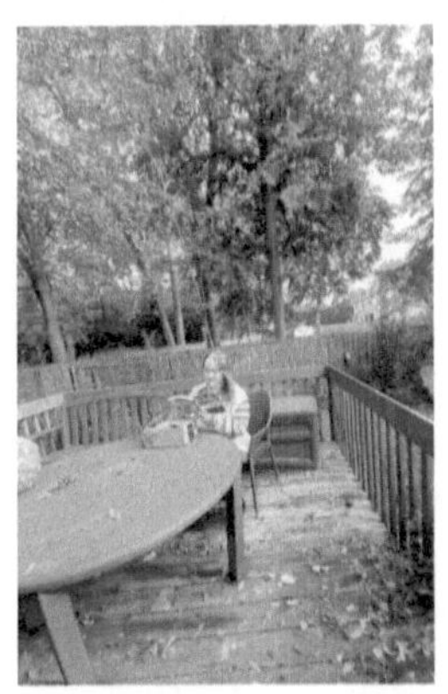

It's the evening air of—*I finally aced the math test after having to spend many sunny afternoons after school.* The temperature is cool, but warm enough to still sit outside on this early November day. I brush the crunchy brown leaves off the one dry chair after the previous night's rain. The scent of cooking from the nearby homes fills my senses. And tonight, just like all those years ago, I reflect on the approaching holiday season, creative flames kindling within me in anticipation of the magic and hope my favorite time of year holds.

# The Way I See Us

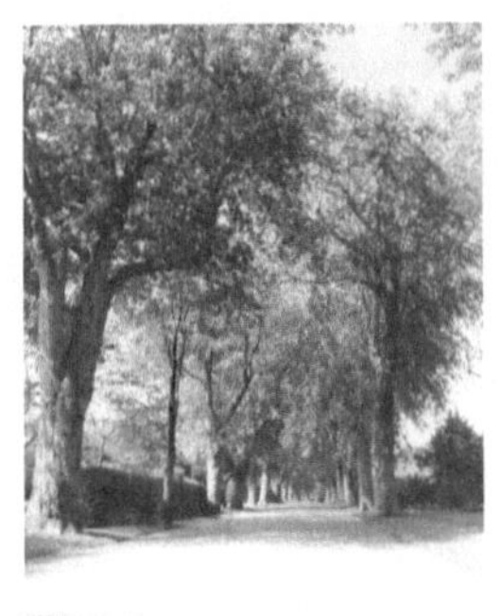

The way I see us,
You can call on me any hour.
You say I am your dream girl,
Well, I can tell you that I never forgot about you.
I'm always ready to pick up right where we left off,
No matter how long you leave.
I'm stuck on you.

You're stuck on me.
And that is wonderful, I say.
To be held onto.
To have someone to always show your heart to.
This is rare and precious.
And if we each, one day, meet someone else,
If we never align in the same place and time,
Or, if we become lovers as we dream;
No matter which way our lives turn,
You will forever have a piece of me.
The way I see us,
We have always been beyond definition.
And to me, we will always be,
Timeless.

# ENVY

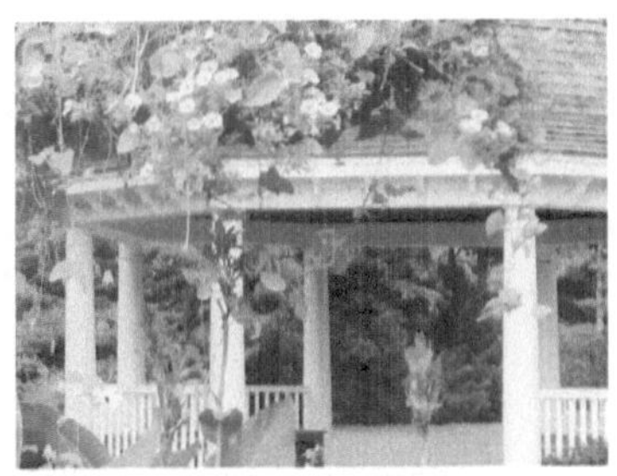

My heart feels heavy tonight.
He got down on bended knee and proposed to you.
Oh, and the way he held you close and stroked your
hair,
and the way you trembled
with genuine, unmistakable joy.
I'm happy for you,
I really am.

But I can't stop the ache in my throat,
the tears wanting to push through,
the insecure feeling that I am not living my life as well
as you,
to be unequivocally loved in that one specific way.

# Laser Focus

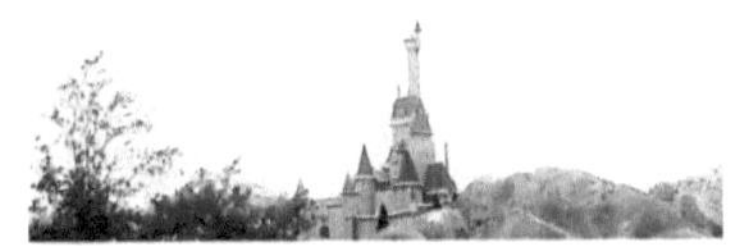

I have a laser focus on my dreams,
Moving with the pangs in my heart
Dripping caffeine into my soul,
Blocking out what I thought I wanted so.
I am passionately exhilarated.
Every day I am driving toward many purposes.
I am heavenly guided.
I am absorbed in bright energy and love-filled emotion.

A feeling that's like diving into the Caribbean Sea
While a New York winter lingers
On the opposite side of me.

# Imprinted on My Heart

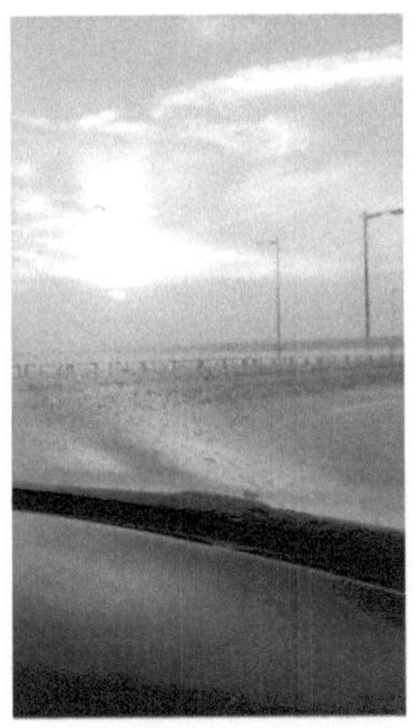

Your soul is imprinted on my heart,
Where all that is precious to my story can be recalled.
I listened to your prayers,
When you were already at an age for judgment to easily
be cast.

You deeply cared for your little brother,
An old soul you were.
You showed me the art you were making.
I bought you a journal hoping you would never
change.
Now you are the age I was then,
And I wish for you to still be the same passionate soul,
A bright being,
Pursuing every goal that is authentic to the unique
spirit I had known.

# TO REMEMBER

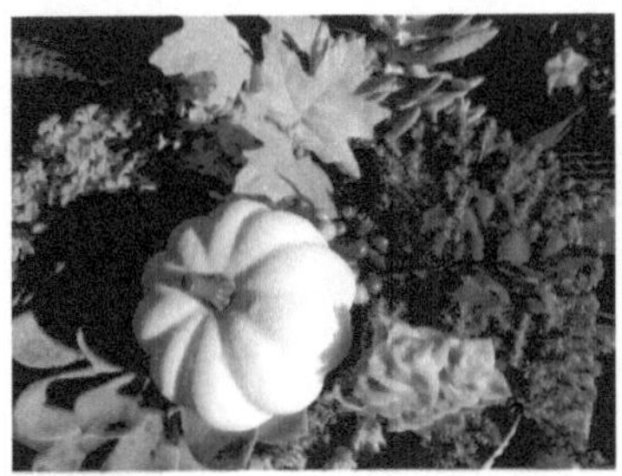

I want to soak this time into my memory,
As leaves, every few minutes, dance down from still-
full trees.
I want to commit the cranberry and gold color to my
heart,
And sunny sweatered days in the backyard
Under cerulean blue skies with lightly feathered
clouds,

As I dream of the celebration of one single day, Thanksgiving,
My soul is immersed in gratitude beyond any autumn season before.

# EXQUISITE

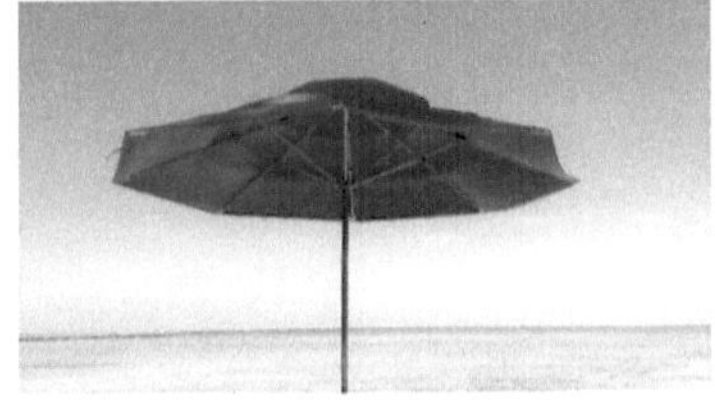

Exquisite,
Like a heart open as a child's.

Exquisite,
As the words off your lips when you see that first pink
and orange sunset with your love.

Exquisite,
Like the taste of a citrus-infused dessert wine.

Exquisite,
As the purest but most passionate connection between
two souls.

# LOVE IS REAL

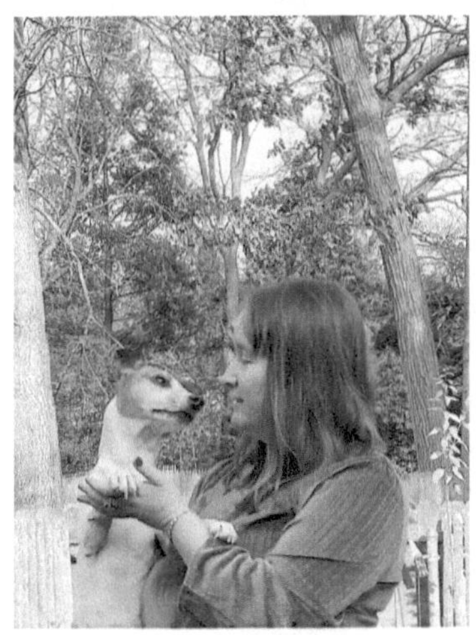

I saw a story on the news last night, about a woman one hundred and five, running a race. The attention didn't faze her much as the newscaster beamed at the finish line. Her mind and heart had a fixed place somewhere else for some time now. Her soul remained tied to him, her beau who passed away far too many years ago. Like young love having never faded; at the mere mention of him, anyone tuned in could feel the tug of her going back, aching for time alone, just the two of them. Her face instantly changed to a blank expression for this world and she drifted off to the man who sang her to sleep each night, who loved her like no one else. So today she runs, not to set records; she runs to keep moving so the cracks in her heart from missing him don't widen. Until she can reunite with the deepest love of her life, she is simply fulfilling a promise made to him to live the best she can. With everything she does, she lives for him, until her dream of the happiest ending and eternal beginning comes true, until she is on that fast plane to Heaven to be in his arms once again.

# MOTHER AND DAUGHTER

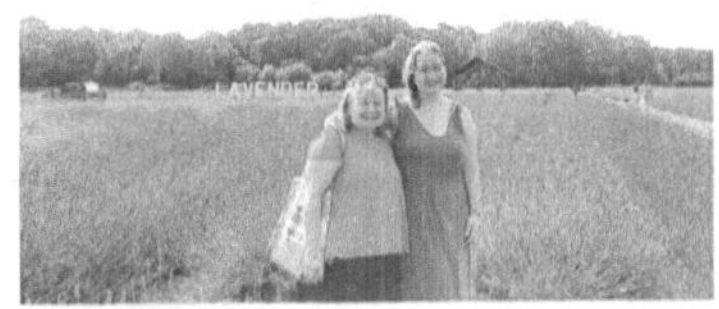

Our spirits are woven together with purple and rose thread. That is why your joys are mine, as well as your sorrows and lingering ghosts. Sometimes your emotions of heartbreak are even heavier for me because of my deep love for you. And,

I am only complete when I live within the heart space of our spirits, unmistakably woven together with purple and rose thread.

# My Perfect Complement

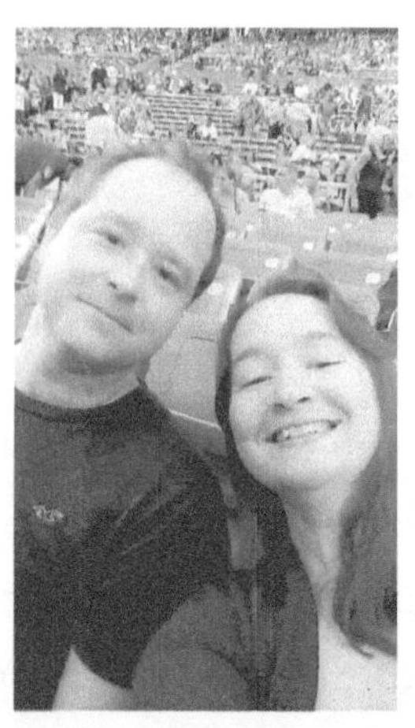

My brother,
You know me the best.
Past my fears,
Beyond my blocks,

Showering me in fresh belief,
To keep me reaching.

# THROUGH THE PAST

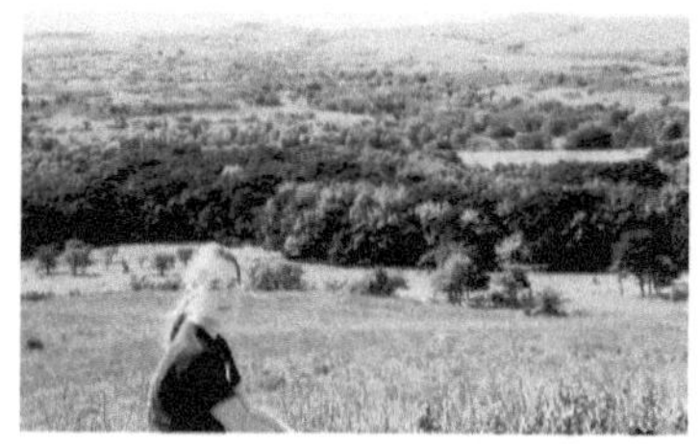

If I could go back in time,
To you sitting on that bench,
So casually cool with your cigarette in hand,
Yet your eyes sparkled when you saw me coming down
the path.
I guess I kind of knew,
But I wasn't sure.
I was always wanting to be sure.
If I could go back,

Maybe I would have sat down closer to you.

Maybe I would have left my apartment ten minutes
earlier,

To have more time to talk with you.

I gravitated to you each day,

Hoping no one else would be near you when I arrived.

If I could go back,

I would be sure.

And you,

You would ask me out.

If only we could go back,

And live within this clearer lens,

To have another chance.

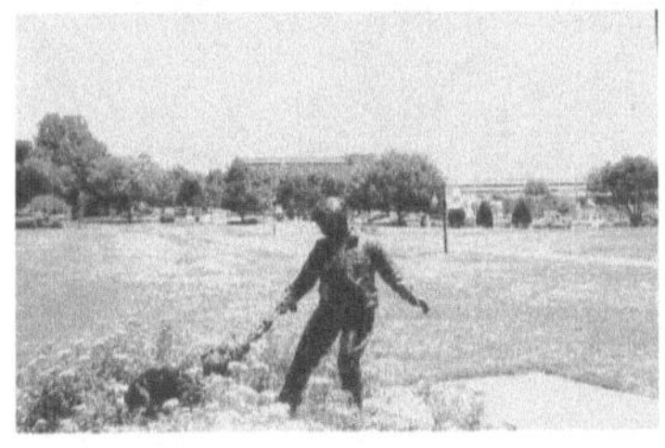

# MARIAH AND TAYLOR

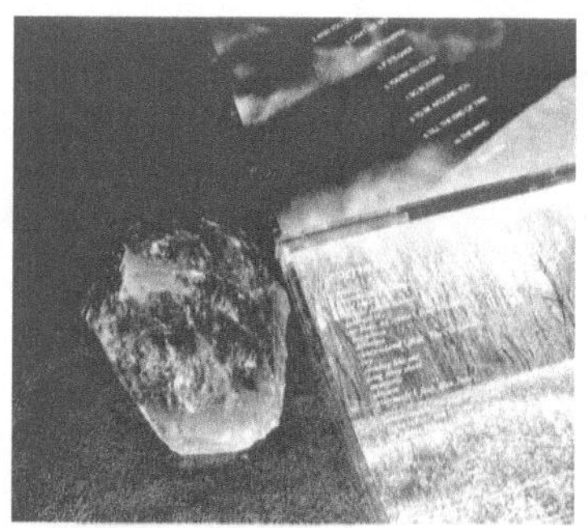

This is my ode to you.

I grew through your art.

Fire signs just like me,

Most people didn't connect with you right away.

But there was a beat you heard just like me,

And this lullaby melody you had to sing;

Words that cried out to be said.

This is where our lives take hold.
This is the safe and right place for people like us.
Within this heart,
And soul,
In the soft, reflective voice,
In the powerful high notes,
We have a never-ending, bright-beaming childhood light,
Thoughts filled with technicolor, ring pops, and the truest love.
I thank you both for holding on, creating the sound-tracks that inspire many of my own sights and feelings to this day.
I thank you for never giving up when others tried to break you down.
These people do try to break us down,
Because we have the nerve to put our hearts out there.
But as you both know,
Art is the most powerful expression.
Love radiates beyond hate.
With a lighter held up to the black sky on a cool summer night,
A sparkle of passion lives forever in the hearts touched,
Like the sparkle lives on in me from listening to both of you.
With the passing decades,

Your souls never changed.

Thank you.

# WHY YOU STAY

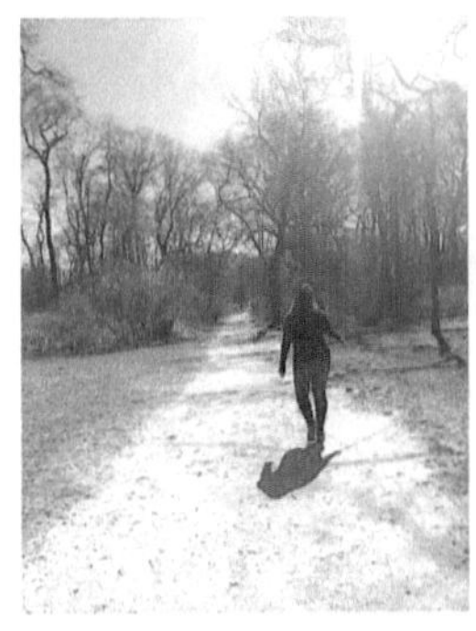

You picked out songs for me.

You dressed up for me.

You held on to me.

You took a picture of the first snow for me.

You stayed up late at night as I read some of my inner words to you.

You never forgot me.
It is all these memories and more,
Truly the smallest of actions that will keep me forever
gratefully tied to you.

# BIRTH OF A STORY

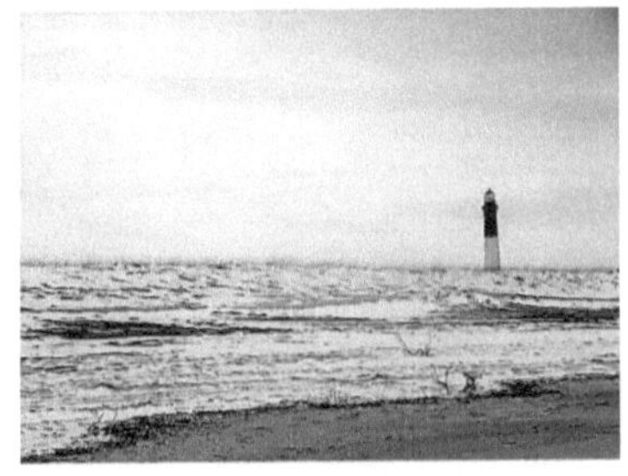

Early morning,

The teal Long Island Sound,

Soon to turn light blue,

The dark blue clouds remain,

The night hasn't left quite yet,

One lone star rests in the sky.

A yellow diamond sun shines up above the brush,

Rising,
An icy chill pierces the heart,
Everything new is everywhere,
Someone is calling.

# Unpopular Thoughts

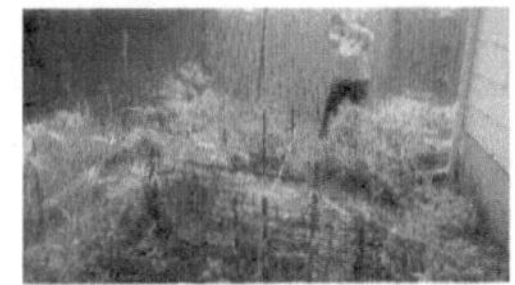

Unpopular thoughts of mine,
These feelings break me down at times,
This belief of mine that personal accomplishments and
art should be acknowledged the same as births, engage-
ments, and marriages.
I can't stop pleading questions of how far we've come
if life keeps being created, and pairings locked in,
without any individual identities being grown,
No unique passions being sown.
Why is it that most only come out for the artists, with

tears in their eyes, when they have departed from this
earthly place?
But these are questions that will continue to be
unanswered,
Since I realize that these are thoughts that will only be
absorbed by the people who already feel the same as
I do.

# Quick to Fall in Love

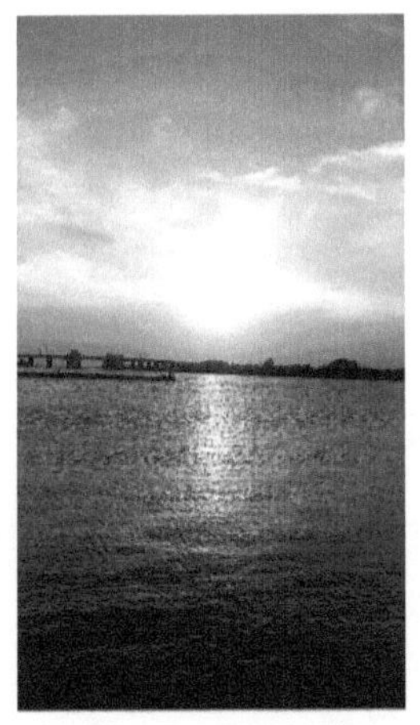

How much time justifies strong feelings?
My heart burned, hearing the way they mocked you.
I've become attached through a single conversation.
Sometimes the connection takes months,
But never years.

And yet, these same people who judge,
They hold lighters up to the term *love at first sight.*
You are never going to know every facet,
Every detail of another human being.
We are all constantly changing and evolving.
But the heart,
The attractive soul,
It's either there or not,
That is what has most of us falling in love,
And that doesn't take long at all.

# THE POWER OF YOUR LOVE

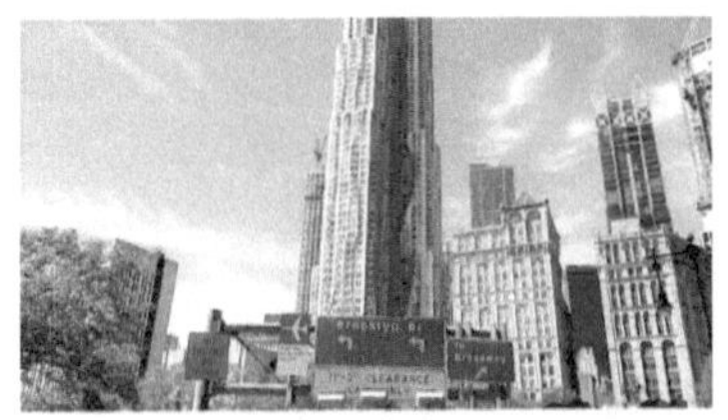

"Remember, you are amazing."
Do you have any idea the holes of pain you lifted her
from with this simple phrase?
This was something you didn't have to say.
There was no incentive for you to tell her this truth.
The statement felt like a goodbye,
And yet,
It's as if you took her hand with this wish,
And walked her down the aisle to her future—

A vision you could see before her.
And you belonged in this position beside her,
only given to one who had proven their love was the
greatest and truest kind.

# A Meaningful Life

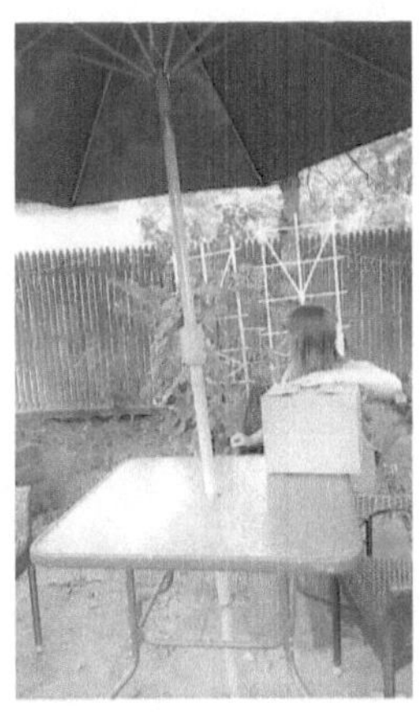

At the end of the day,
Your love gave meaning to my life.
Yes, your love gave meaning to my life.
We didn't need to be a match for me to care for you.

When dreams and wins are shared, received, and
adored by another,
Striving to be your best becomes a lifelong act of love,
To honor the treasures another saw in you.

# CAMEO

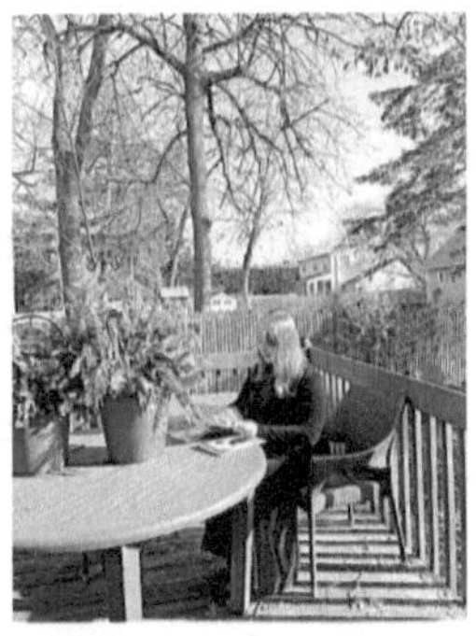

Reflecting on the lives I made part of my story for a
while:
The walks together down foreign suburbia blocks,
Fancy rooftop dinners in the sparkling city where
thoughts were focused upon what fork to use,
The drive to the farm to meet his family in an old

country house filled with problems far greater than
my own,
but love,
powerful love that could undoubtedly overcome all
odds,
Rocking a baby boy to sleep, feeling the weight of
responsibility and treasure I held,
And being younger and older within my heart in
varying places and times—
All these lives and moments were touched till fate
decided which road my journey was to take me down
next.
But these cameo memories will never be left behind.
These times are forever embossed on my heart,
And they will always be part of the tapestry of
passionate shades that make me who I am today.

# LEARNING FROM REGRETS

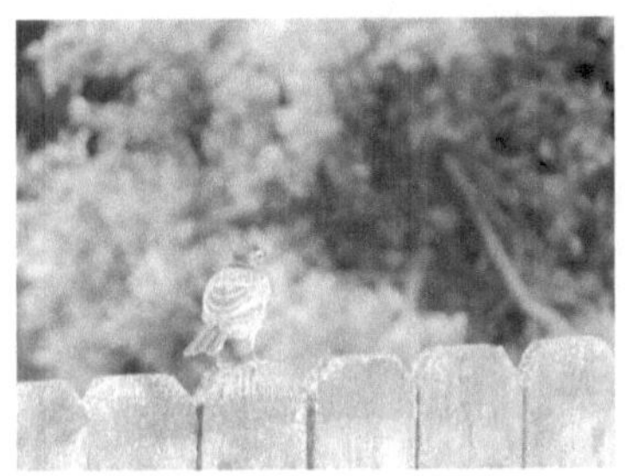

To cowardice moments past,
when I should have overcome my own hurt in the
name of love,
I remember you all.

To be strong is virtuous and lasting,
bestowing peace in whichever outcome fate and
destiny decide,

and why—in steps forward—I will strive for bravery's side.

# Never Changing

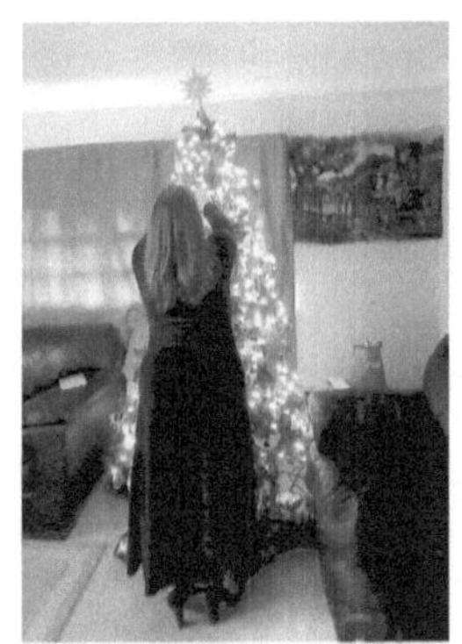

A romantic soul,
candied heart,
will always believe.

# ROMANCE ME

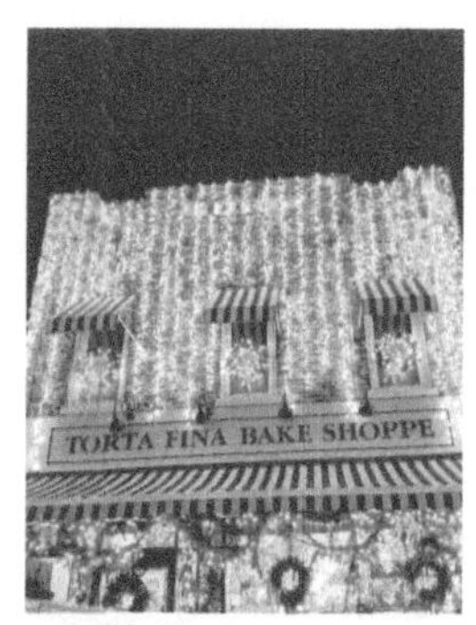

Roses—
Are my favorite,
Bright red on white linen,
Stem candles glowing beside you,
My Love.

# TAKING ON TWO-YEAR-OLD ME

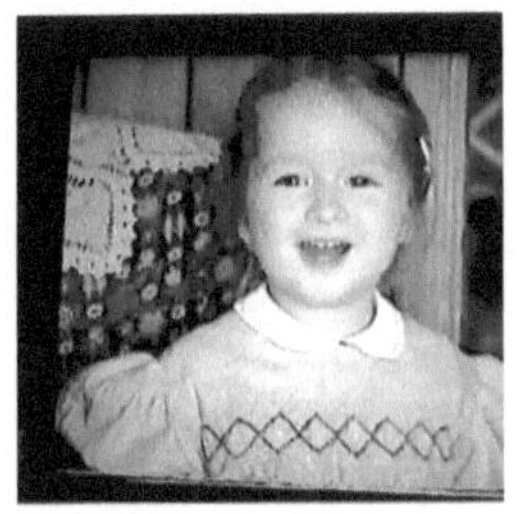

Two-year-old me would be excited to see all the cars around her—
Red, Blue, and *"Whoa! Look At That Bright Green One!"*
She wouldn't get her face all red from a traffic jam.
She'd imagine magical tracks being slipped under the car so they could fly above all the others through the clouds.

Why not?
She would love to be in charge at the wheel,
Navigating her ship
With a sailor's cap on,
Feeling proud of all that she is.

# Impressions

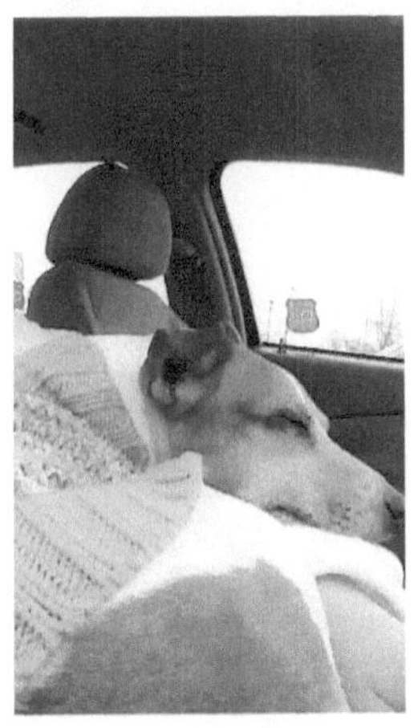

Angry voices
Slamming doors
Veiled threats
Masked and upfront insults

But also—

Special cd-track dances beside the rainbow-lit
Christmas tree
Long, soul-inspiring drives along the Ocean Parkway
A bracelet from you with your sentiment—
"So you always know what you deserve."

# A WIDE-OPEN WORLD

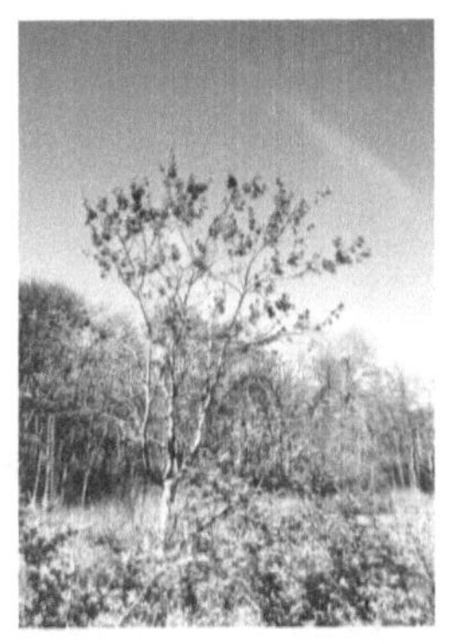

A break from the material world,
Eyes are clearer,
Brightened by an early November snow.
Vision is avant-garde,
Noticing an Autumn Blaze Maple with satin-looking,

delicate bright cherry leaves meticulously poised on
branches,
Imagining a dress of simply this over bare skin.

# Solar Return

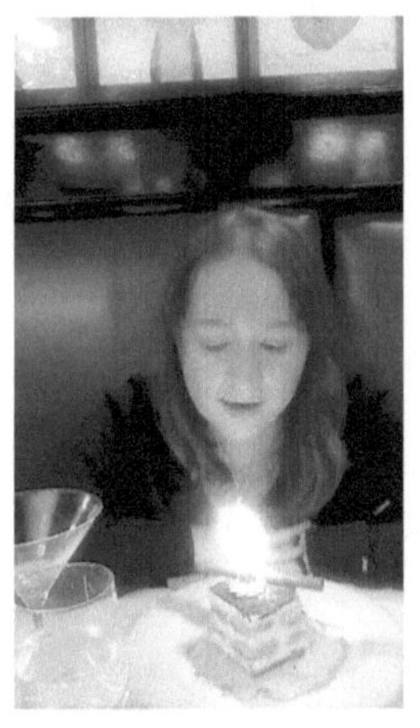

A cord suddenly pulled in me.
I discovered I desperately needed time to re-see,
To press pause and truly focus on more of the woman I
desire to be.

I realize there is no magical key,
Only a valued family tree,
And wishes stirring with heart-aching ferocity inside
of me.

# THE LOVE I REQUIRE

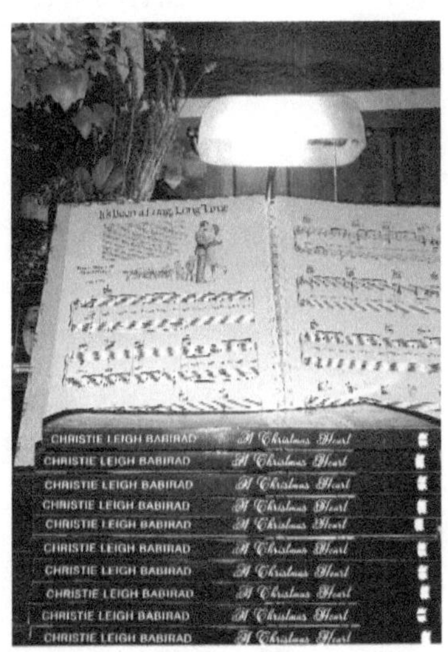

I want a love I long to jump into,
like a child into a pool on a hot summer day.

I want a love that knows each other inside and out, but
there are still sweet surprises,
like a full rainbow in the sky after a week of storms,
alive with happy tears,
singing out, "I really am the luckiest one."
I want a love that has me reaching,
yet adores me the way I am.
The love I want is not a fantasy, despite what skeptics
raise,
and it is a love worth waiting for.
Anything less, for me, is not worth anything at all.

# CHRISTMAS TIME

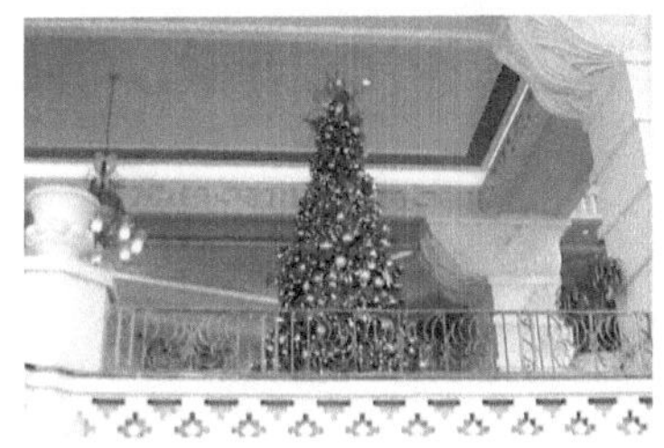

Looking back now
I remember it all
when a chocolate a day
meant Santa would soon be on his way.

Green and Red paper chains
Wrapped around our tree.
Mom loved them because they were made by me.

Holly Leaf Cookies,
Jolly rancher color sticking to my fingers—
it's the scent that lingers.

Emerald trees strewn with sparkling silver,
angels in the snow,
tingling from my head to my toes.

# POINT OF ENTRY

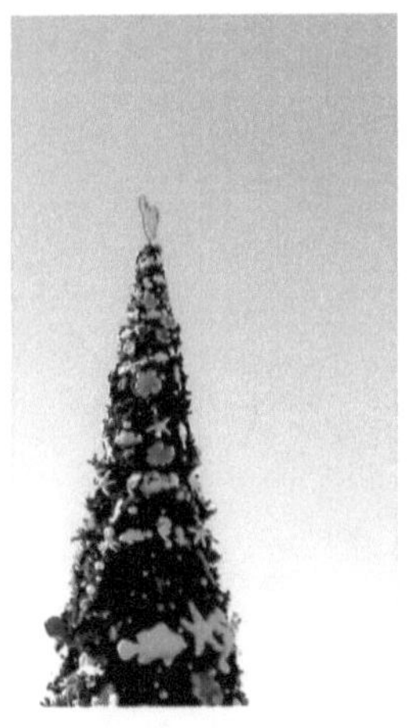

When the dance was billowing gowns,
Passionate movement
Of fairies, princesses, and the most dashing and caring
princes.
To go back,

To watching the snow slowly fall,
Standing outside in the middle of it all.
Imagining in this world you truly can become anything
at all.
Maybe I must go back,
To break these chains of time I wrapped around the
most authentic pieces of me.
Maybe this freed spot is exactly where I need to
approach my new year,
My point of entry to the life I have always dreamed of.

# HOLIDAY TIME

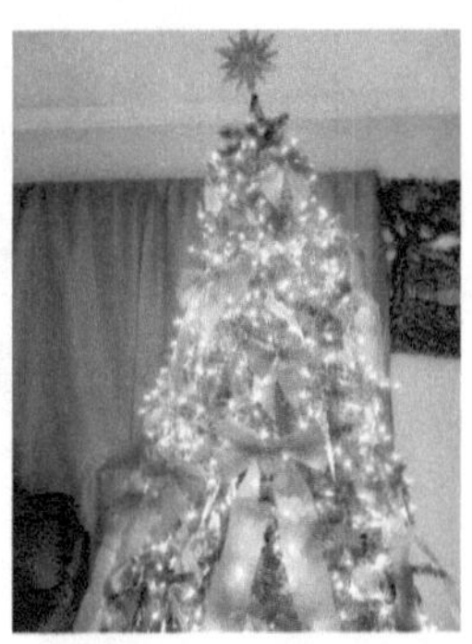

Warm, white-lit, red-bowed Christmas tree,
Strawberry hot chocolate,
Winter walk,
Jack Frost staying on my nose;
And with the first snowfall,
I slide swiftly into this slowed-down, cozy sweater-
weather, precious time of year.

# MUSICAL STORIES

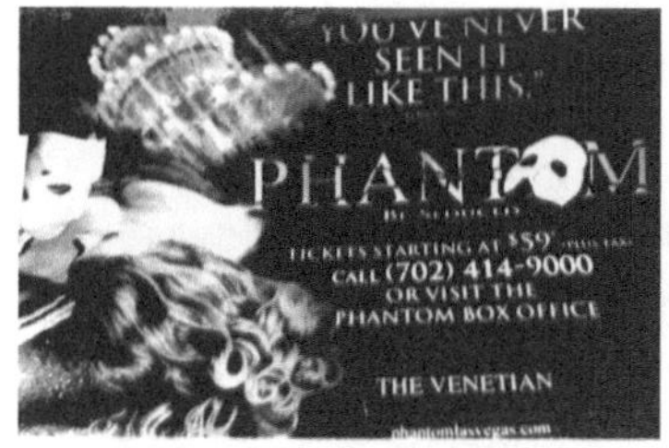



Strings of musicals play.
In lost times they take on even greater resonance.
Classics that shaped me in my formative years,
Set to full-piece orchestras.
Visceral imagery locked like a small shiny golden key to
a teenage diary,
Raw with truth and impossible to replicate heart.
I've taken in stories of men who love their ladies with
timeless love, courage, pride, song, and dance.

The Sound of Music and Phantom of The Opera
are two,
Guiding lights in the power of storytelling and music
lifted together into the most star-filled night.

# SITTING DOWN WITH CHLOE

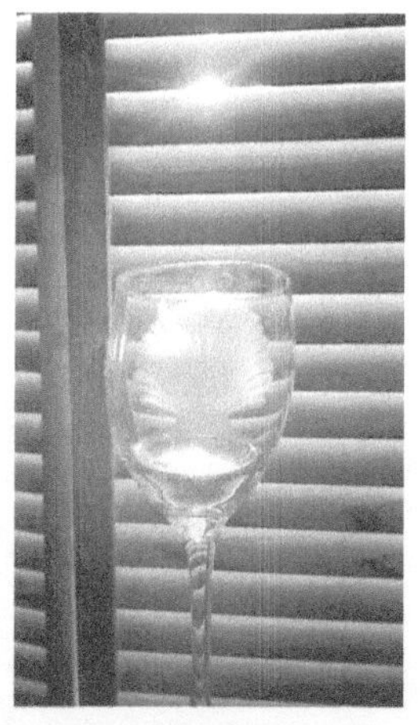

My emotions,
I must sit down with you and have a chat.
We are not going to have you getting the best of me
like that.
The joy, the laughter, the silliness,

That is all still here.

Look at how he is still bossing you around with his high-pitched bark in your ears.

Yes, I know these test results bring us down each year,

But look at the way he cocks his head as the tears fall down your face—

Right now, he simply can't understand why you won't just get up with him and play.

To love so profoundly will always be accompanied by inevitable loss.

When the time comes, the pain will undeniably pour with a force greater than ever before,

But you're going to keep perspective front and center this time.

You are going to keep the joy, the laughter, the silliness, and all the memories with you.

You will know this is only a temporary state.

We will all be together again one day.

And you will continue to love.

You can't deny yourself the greatest pleasure and purpose of this life.

So, Chloe, My Dear, it's time you dry your eyes and get outside.

We need to live and play, and the rest will work itself out no matter which way.

# DREAMS

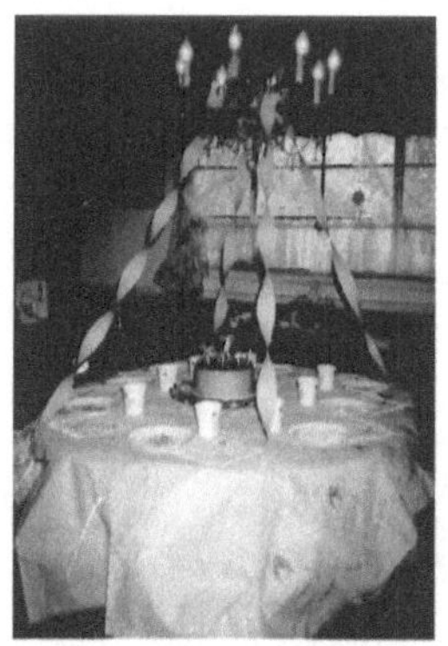

Where do dreams come from, not the ones you wish
but the ones that come as you fall asleep at night?
There are witches at my front door, and falling from a
chair into a bottomless, water-filled abyss. But there are
also blue owls and foxes that come as clear friends.
They stop and stare. The foxes sometimes run with

me, away from the dangerous, tangled tree-limbed woods. They both seem to emphasize a message for me to continue following my own path and to stay away from that which contradicts my identity. They warn with their focus upon me that this will always be a present threat. Then, there are sometimes visitors who have left my life or long since passed on from our earthly place. I try to hold on. I tell them to please stay, but they always go away in a cloud of smoke, or as my eyes suddenly open and my heart steadies to incomplete normalcy, trying to remember the single statement they came to relay.

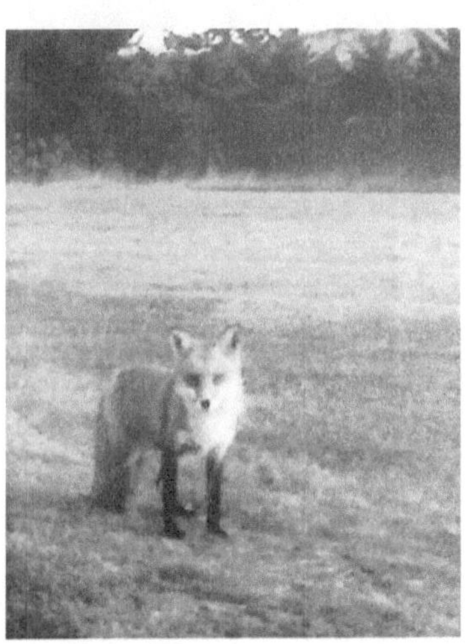

# Ballerina

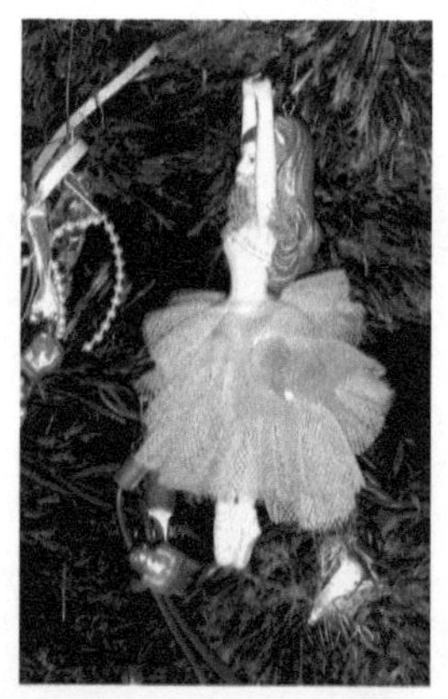

A symbol of greatness.
Poised strength,
Passion through music,
Ethereal costumes,
Sleek leotards,
And soft, iridescent ballet shoes,

Contrasting the intense work required of every muscle.
Perseverance and love for art melding,
The ballerina is a depiction of the human spirit,
Everlasting on the heart and exquisite in detail,
It's no wonder Degas chose this as his prime subject of
inspiration.

# THE WAY DESTINY GOES

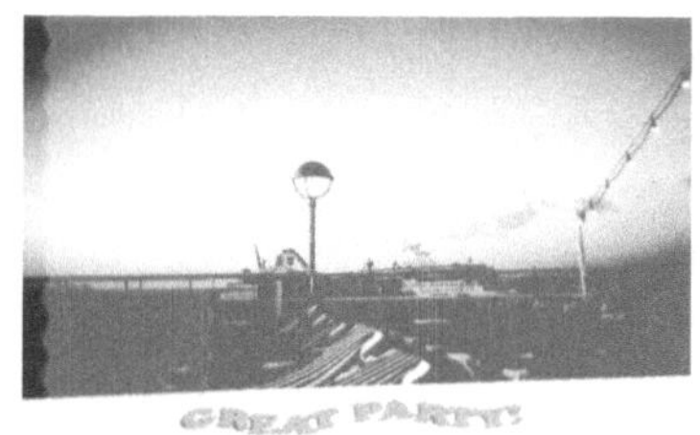


Destiny woven into years,
Through unplanned days,
Waving a stick of bright summer-colored streamers in
the air.
The sparkled legacy,
Created amid the most authentic and uninhibited
seasons.
What you've been wanting and waiting for,
Reaching you always in what feels like the nick of time.

# FOR MY WRITING

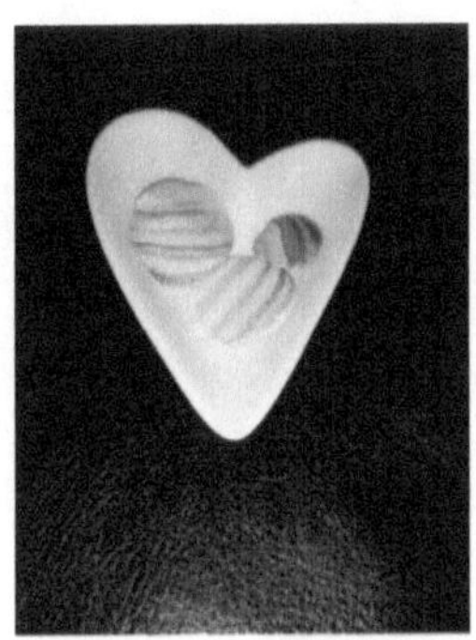

I search for a story that will change a life,
Trickling down an overheated body like rain on an
early August night,
A story that will stay on the mind long after the tale
has been read,
Sliding swiftly down into the heart

Like the shiny purple and white wampum shells to
their ocean bed,
A treasure reminding one someone,
*"You are here for a unique reason that goes far beyond
any tough season."*

# PROGRAMMED FOR TRUE LOVE

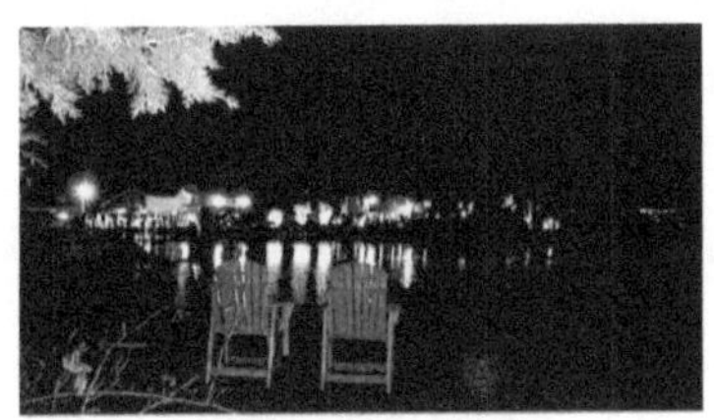

I accidentally dropped the movie ticket stub.
He hurried to pick the piece of paper up.
*"I'll hold on to it,"* he said gruffly.
And in that one reaction I knew,
We were done.


The single dirty utensil left on the table after dinner,
The plate pushed to the center when finished for
someone else to clean,
The napkin given with no "thank you" when received,

Walking ahead of me,
Wandering off without a single explanation,
Unlocked doors,
Slamming shower doors,
Drawers left broken,
A face's worth of shaving cream left on sink handles;
It is all these subtle memories and more that I am now
grateful for.

Growing up, many of us are taught to simply let these
frustrations go,
When our instincts are screaming, *"This is wrong!"*
But I've been taking all of these moments in and to
heart, and I realize—
I was being programmed for true love all along.
Warning alarms now sound within me when I witness
the all-too-familiar signs.
If this is it, I would rather be alone.
But I don't believe that this is it.
We all deserve so much more.

# HOME

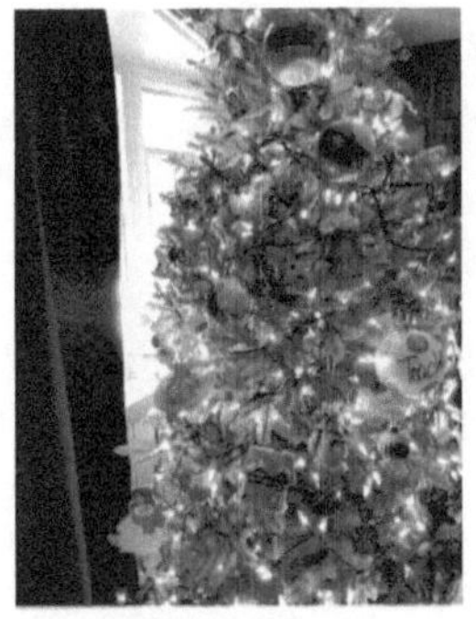

Home is an array of sentimental pieces in the heart,
Like storied ornaments on a Christmas tree,
And therefore, cannot be whittled down by a singular
place on the map you see.

# A Call for Lace

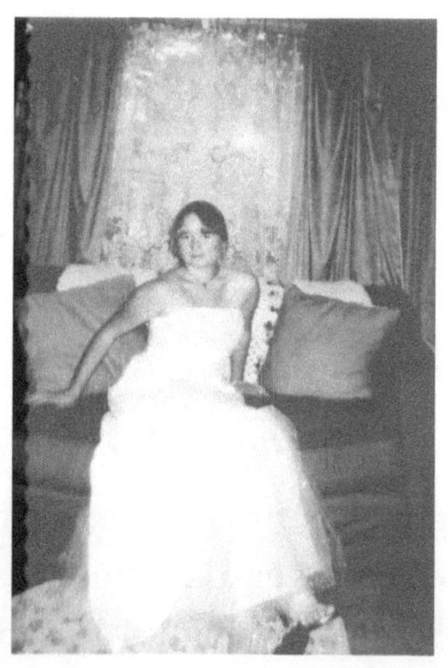

Lacey things,
A man reacts to

This soft touch,
Delicate,
A symbol of another side,
Where life is slower and cherished.

# Sense Memory

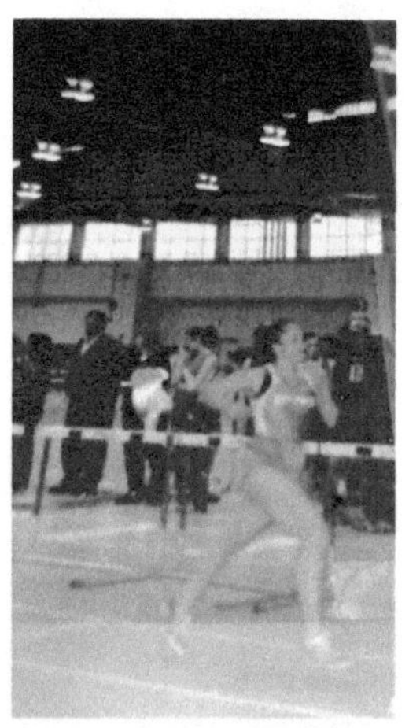

Rain on my heavy nylon, royal blue Winter Track coat,
Cold biting air on the nape of my bare neck,
Pavement black sky,

Scents of exhaust from cars mixed with diner food
cooking nearby,
The large building's gymnasium lights;
Swish went our pants.
A team of girls facing our competitors with exhilara-
tion pounding in our hearts,
And in our heads, there was almost tangible belief that
tonight could change absolutely everything.

# THE RIGHT SONG

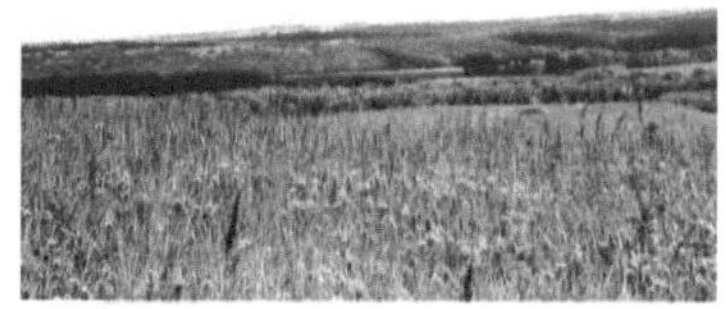

The right song takes you down the road immediately,
To open land beyond what the eyes can see,
Has your hand to your heart, feeling as if it could leap
right out of your chest,
Because you're taking in what you thought was
completely gone,
You're hearing a voice and melody that captures what
you've always wanted,
and so much more.

# METAPHOR FOR THE MOMENT

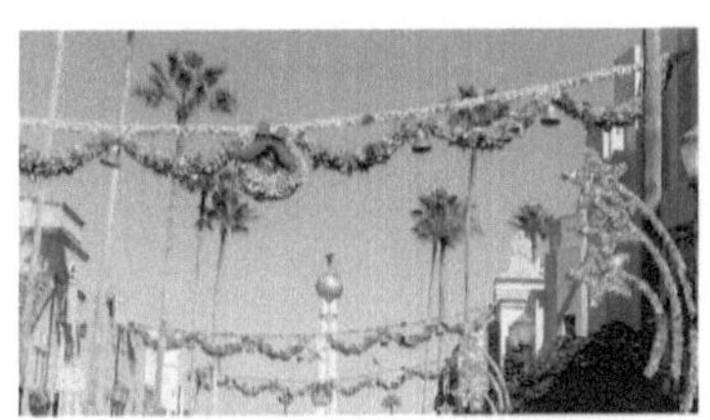

Stop the ride,

I want to get off!

The days are passing way too fast,

And I think I missed the ring at the last attraction.

# A Night to Hold Onto

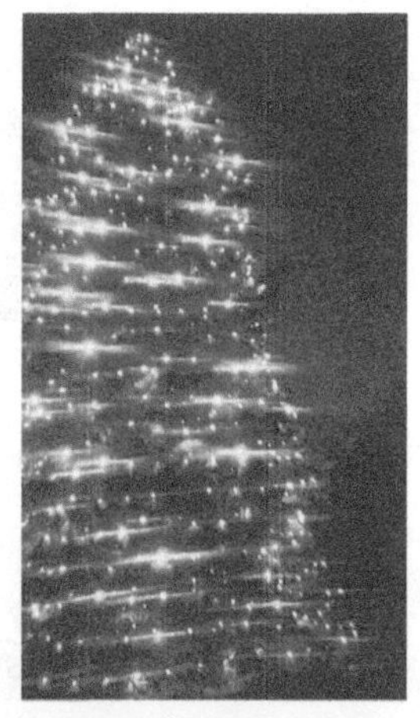

What a magical night!
I wish it would never end.
Maybe if I stay here with you a little bit longer
Next to the candy-colored lit village tree
Beneath this evening chill,

My hands wrapped inside yours
In the quiet,
Glistening eyes looking into yours,
We won't need a picture to hold onto.
We will have this memory forever in our hearts.
And as each month goes by,
We'll have certainty,
Like stars in the night sky,
We were meant to be.

# Christmas Drives

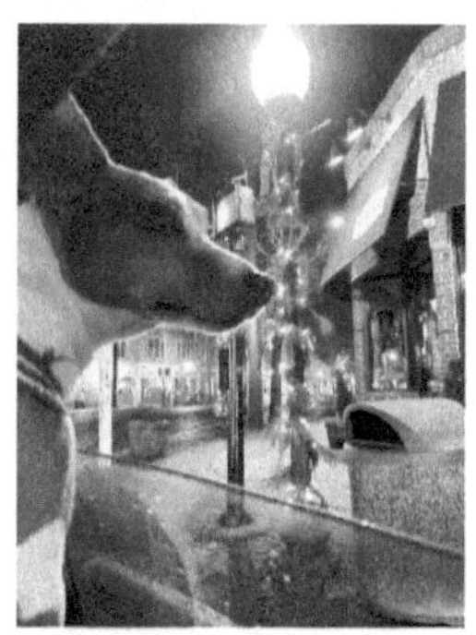

I want to hold onto this season.
I never want to let go of—
Mom driving slow down streets with joyfully lit
homes,
Lampposts aglow with ruby-red bows,
No thoughts ahead,
Time rolling deeply within this season.

My Jack Russell with his head out the window taking
this all in—
His ears straight up in curiosity for the magic that
surrounds this time of year.
And I hope,
Beyond this ache in my heart,
That this sweet tradition will forever remain.

# A Takeover of Darkness

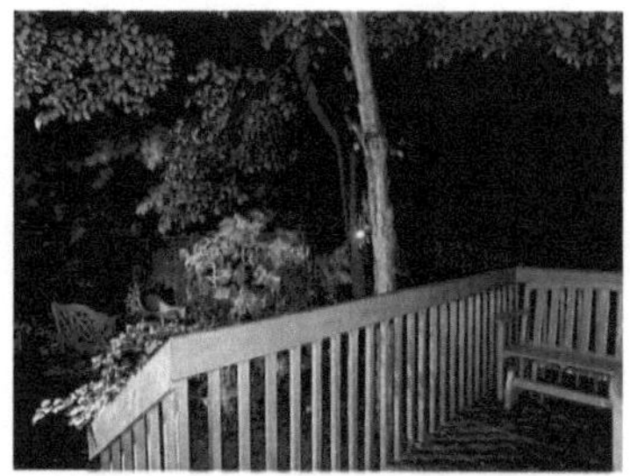

There have been recent times when I've wanted to
leave behind most of humankind.
With news of crimes that rip slow at my optimistic
heart and mind,
It has been difficult to hold onto anything bright and
hopeful I would still often find.

# A Friend

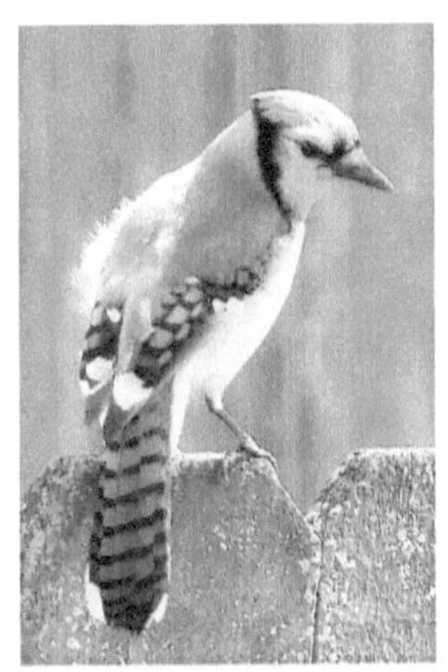

You didn't question me,
Didn't judge.
You trusted I'd find my way.
You didn't surmise answers.
You believed in me like the rising dawn's sun.

My path, you knew, would be discovered,
Within what has never existed before.
I dreamed in the deepest crimson and blue,
And you encouraged with silent love and scarlet tulips,
With each step I took.

# Good News Daily

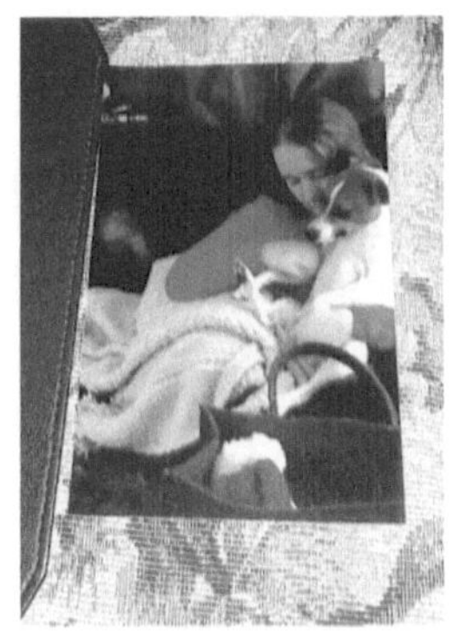

I think many of us wish for a widespread paper that
prints only positive news,
Not stories of animals being saved, because they were
never put in danger in the first place.
We want stories purely of love, laughter, and joy,

and the light that makes this world worth living in
at all.
I, for one, know that this side does, in fact, exist,
And there has never been a more desperate time in
history for tales that fit this particular list.

# The Memory Vault

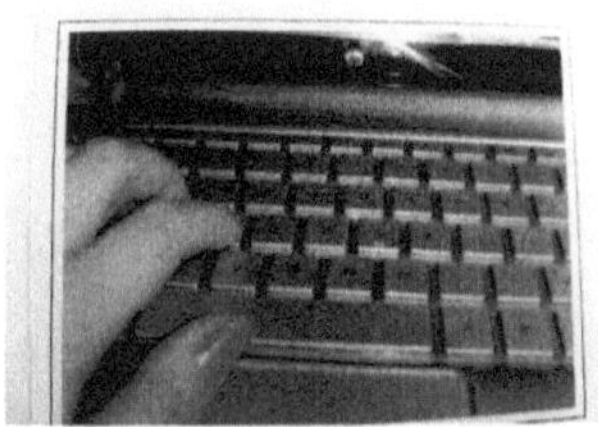


The mind is a powerful force, but it is nothing without feelings.
It is nothing without your memories and the recognition of how spectacularly beautiful those vivid memories are.

When all the days are done, I will remember...

Captree, Long Island—
Walking the boardwalk at night,
Looking at the docked boats,
And shimmering water lit by the lamps and moonlight
with my family.
I will remember that the salt air is strongest here, and
how we would collect the brochures about each boat
out of the plastic mailbox cases.
I will remember how this place never became old.

My dogs,
The kisses they gave when welcoming me home, even if
I had only gone to the grocery store.

Dancing,
In the living room with my mom to Wham's "Last
Christmas."

Art,
The way it felt to hear it, sing it, and write it all out
time and time again.

The Picture,
Of me with the first grown-up purple bike that my
grandfather bought me.

The Sound,
Of my mom playing the piano and organ.

The Feeling,
Of a young child looking up to me, needing me,
wanting to learn from me.

Love,
Every single kind,
Experiencing, observing, and reflecting back upon it.

The Exhilaration,
Of getting lost in a story.

Simple times with friends.

The Scent,
Of chlorine in the very early morning,
And grass and rain.

The adrenaline rush of a race,
Winning when I've put all of my heart and soul into
the movement of my legs.

Nights I get to dress up,
And days I can wear my favorite pajamas all day.

Ocean Parkway drives with Mom.

The room my older brother set up for me the first time living away from home with him—the soft light blue comforter he bought for me.

The way the sky opens up heading west.

The old school rap music my brother and I would play to lighten the heaviness of having to say goodbye when leaving home.

Life is everything with this memory vault, which is still to be filled with so much more.

What is in your memory vault?

# THIS NEW YEAR'S EVE

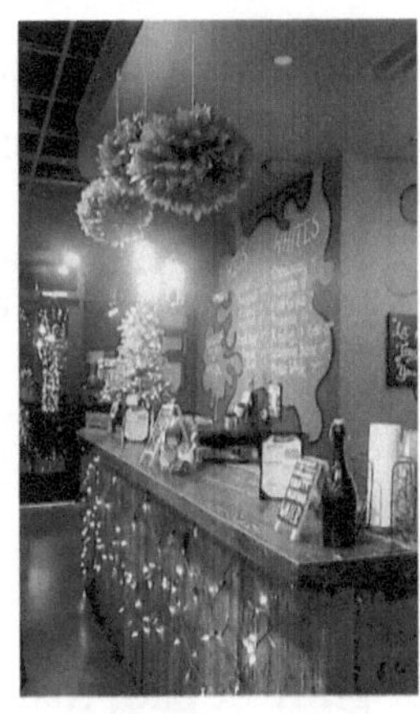

On this New Year's Eve, I pray for the inhumanity to
cease,
But it's a problem so much bigger than I could ever
handle.
Can't stop it,

But I won't let these acidic images in anymore,
Into this all-too-fragile heart.
No more reading those heartbreaking headlines,
I'm fighting back the only way I can,
We can,
On our canvases,
With our paintbrushes,
Ink on notebook pages,
At the theater or music club, singing out through our
microphone,
Even if only one person hears the message.
I still believe in the potential widespread power.
Pounding out our unbeatable belief on those ivory and
black keys,
On this New Year's Eve, this is what I am getting ready
for again.
I am tending to my soul.
I am pushing back the broken.
I am cutting through the brush.
I am creating the brightly lit path that will lead me on
my way.
I know I have this battle for light ahead once again,
For I have seen too much.
I have seen enough of the negative,
Setting me back for far too many seconds in this
precious life.

No more.

I promise you,

I'm going to continue to fight for all of us.

I am moving forward once again,

In this new year.

# WRITER

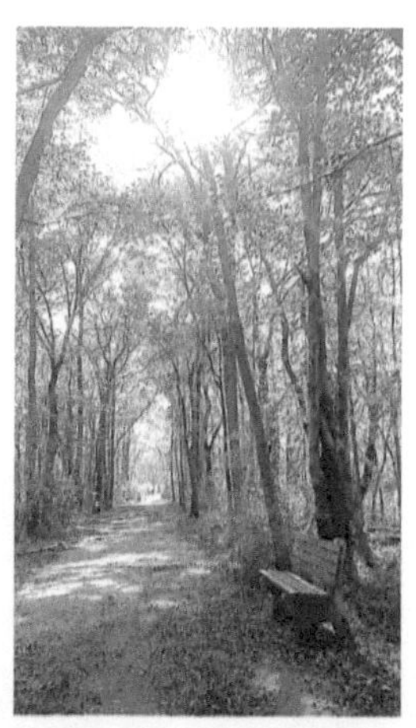

I cut my heart open,
right down the middle,
playing with my greatest fears,
digging up memories that are still raw,
all for the purpose of existing for one other somebody.

# On My Wish List

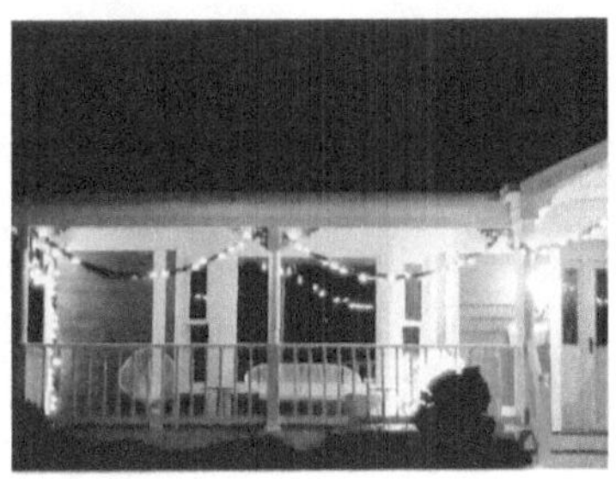

I think I'd like a front porch,
A safe spot to sit and linger for a while,
To have a favorite mug with hot coffee on a chilly night
Under the Christmas lights,
Kissing and holding your hand beneath the moonlight.

# The Results Are In

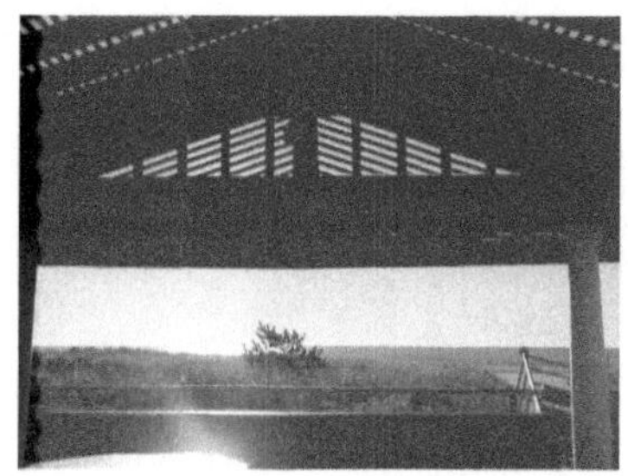

These past couple of years have taught me a lot.
What I thought was forever,
Under no uncertain terms informed me,
We must part.

I learned what love truly means.
The definitions went far beyond my initial dreams.

In these years I lived within the light but mostly dark,
I don't believe there's any other way to emerge,
Like the bright-in-melodious-song Lark.

# Acknowledgments

First and foremost, I would like to thank my family who inspires me daily. You are my home no matter where I go—Mom, Dad, Robbie, Grandma, Grandpa, Alistair and Holly.

I would also like to thank all my close friends and family who have been incredibly supportive of my work. I started to list all of you and then did not want to leave anyone out, but you know who you are and I am so very grateful to have you all in my life. I am truly blessed. Thank you to those of you who have attended my events and enjoyed my books, you are all so special to me. I think anyone who creates art, creates initially from this inner place, but then we all want our works to translate to others. I wish for my words to continue to connect with you and fill your heart with lots of spirit and love.

I also want to thank everyone at Harbor Lane Books, especially Erica for bringing these works of mine out into the world for you all to read and connect with. Finally, thank you to God for giving me such strong faith in that which cannot be seen nor defined but flutters like butterflies inside of me, encouraging me to keep writing with all of my heart and soul.

# About the Author

Christie Leigh Babirad lives on Long Island and is a poetess of numerous collections. She continually aspires to illuminate the moments in life, no matter the size or subject, and create art that will not fade with the passing time.

You can follow her work on social media at the following sites to find out more about her latest projects.

facebook.com/authorchristieleighbabirad

instagram.com/christieleighbabiradauthor

youtube.com/@christieleighbabirad1707

goodreads.com/cbabiradauthor

## ABOUT THE PUBLISHER

Harbor Lane Books, LLC is a US-based independent digital publisher of commercial fiction, non-fiction, and poetry.

Connect with Harbor Lane Books on their website (www.harborlanebooks.com) and social media @harborlanebooks.

facebook.com/harborlanebooks

x.com/harborlanebooks

instagram.com/harborlanebooks

tiktok.com/@harborlanebooks

threads.com/harborlanebooks

pinterest.com/harborlanebooks

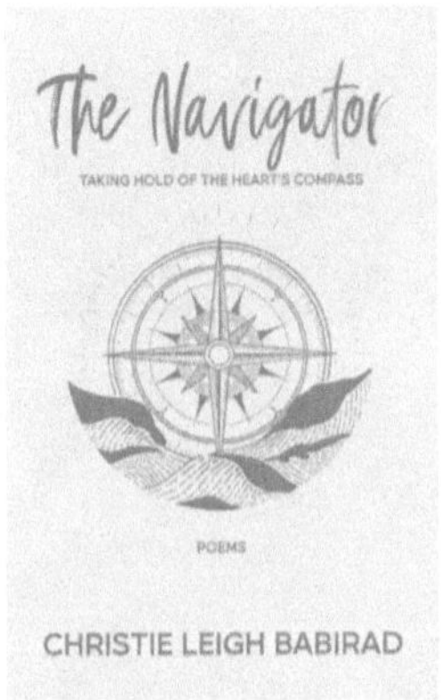

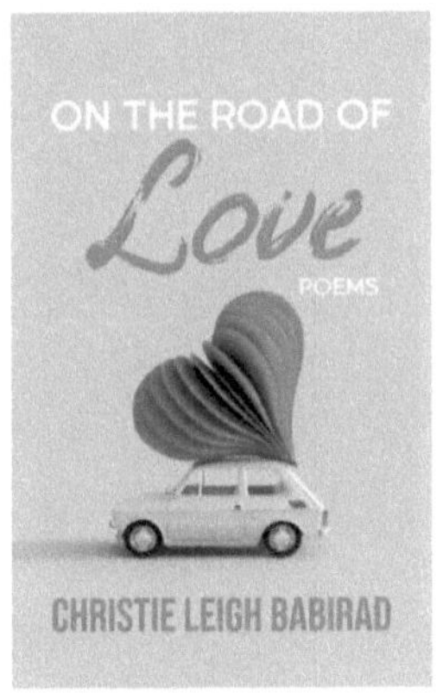

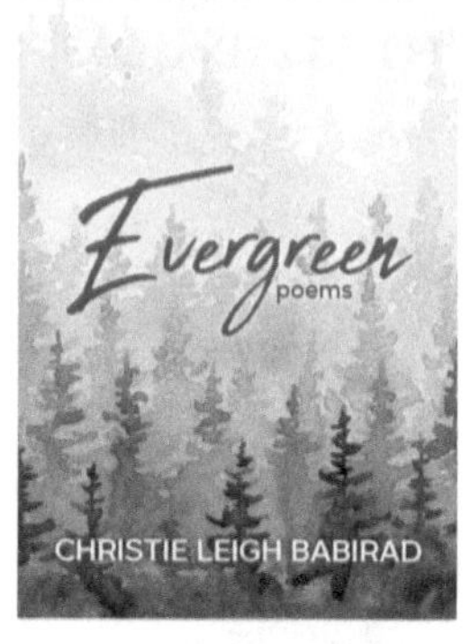

Evergreen
poems
CHRISTIE LEIGH BABIRAD


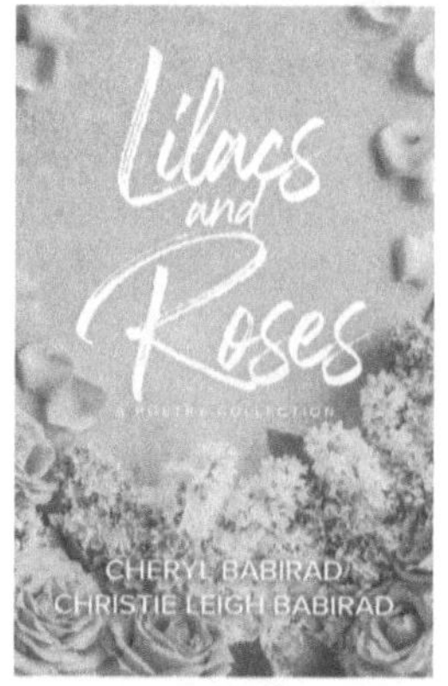

Lilacs
and
Roses
A POETRY COLLECTION
CHERYL BABIRAD
CHRISTIE LEIGH BABIRAD

www.ingramcontent.com/pod-product-compliance
Lightning Source LLC
Chambersburg PA
CBHW030913060726
47591CB00005B/1530